ISBN 9798866916818
Title: candy dandy selfie: Alessandro Chiodo - WORKS

First published in 2023
Edited by Alessandro Chiodo, Münster

Front cover: artwork by Alessandro Chiodo
© VG Bild-Kunst, Bonn 2023

Find out more about the artist:
alessandrochiodo.net

candy dandy selfie

Alessandro Chiodo

WORKS

Pondera Verborum Art Project

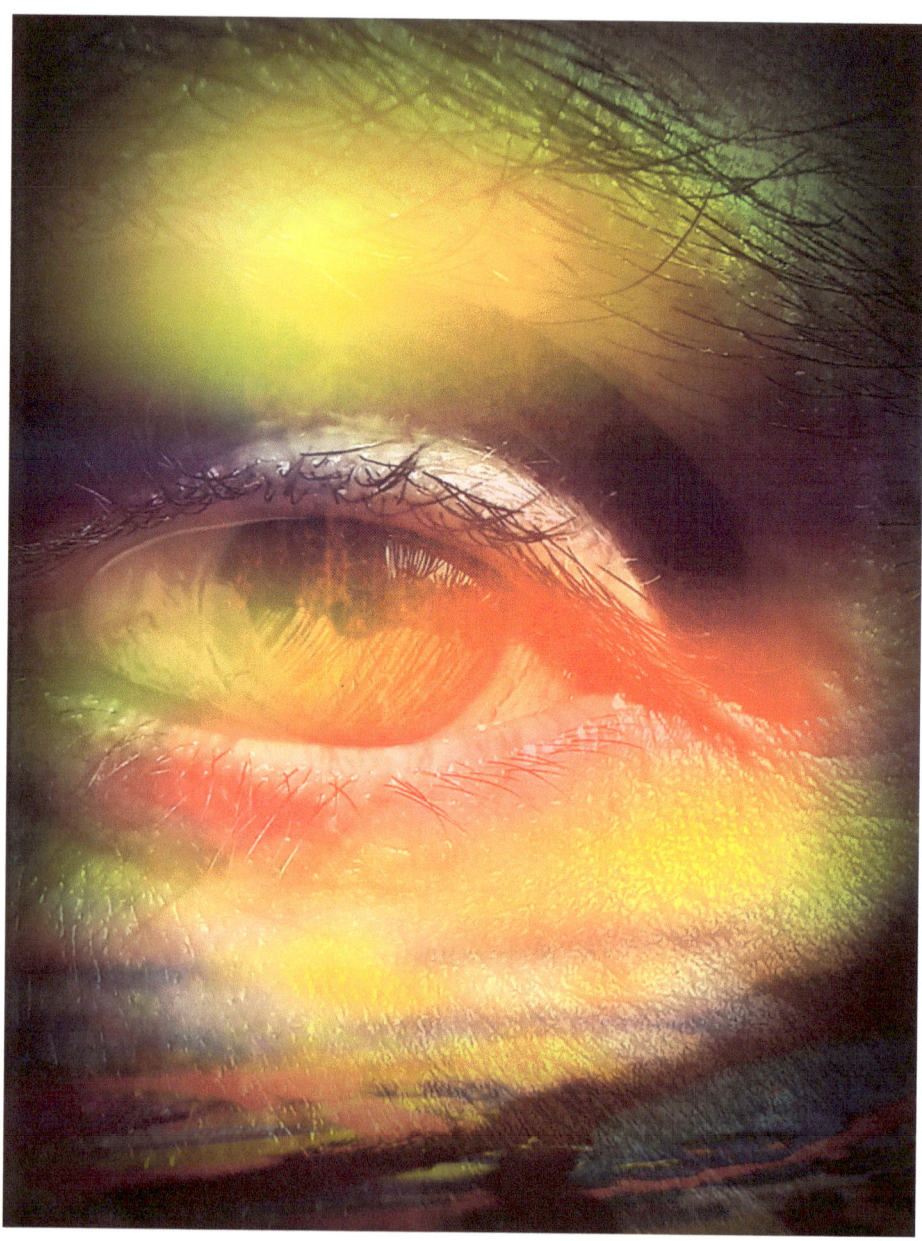

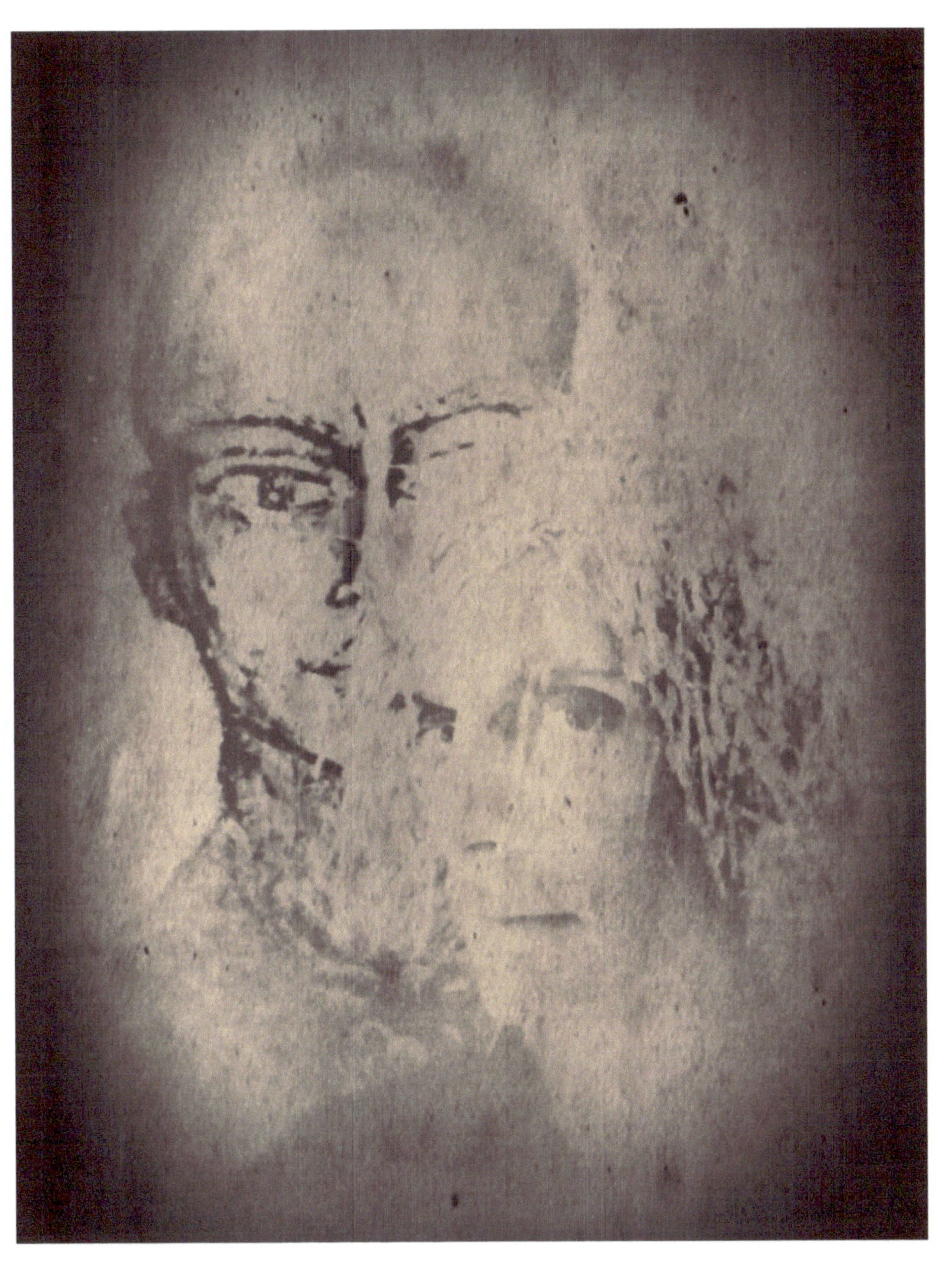

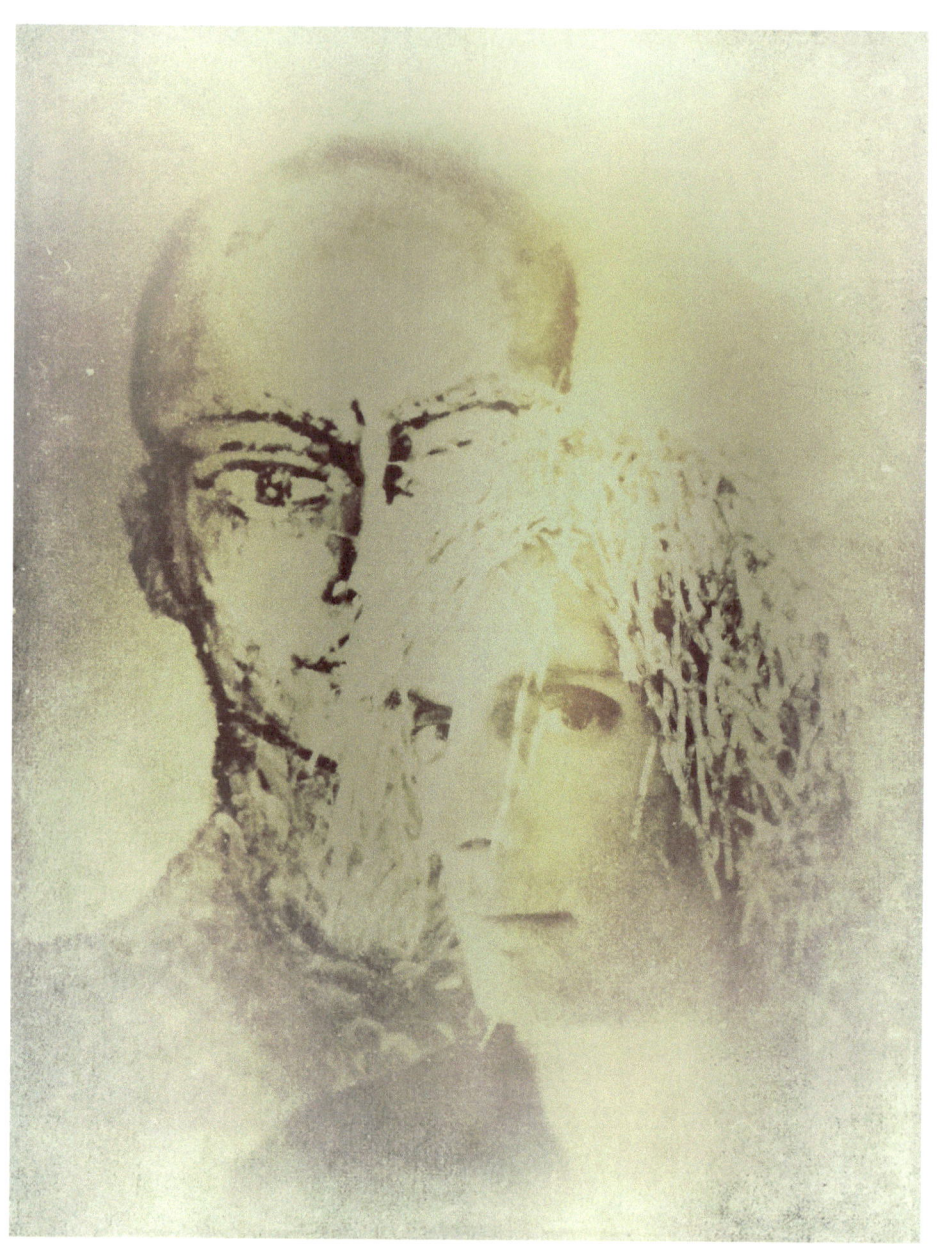

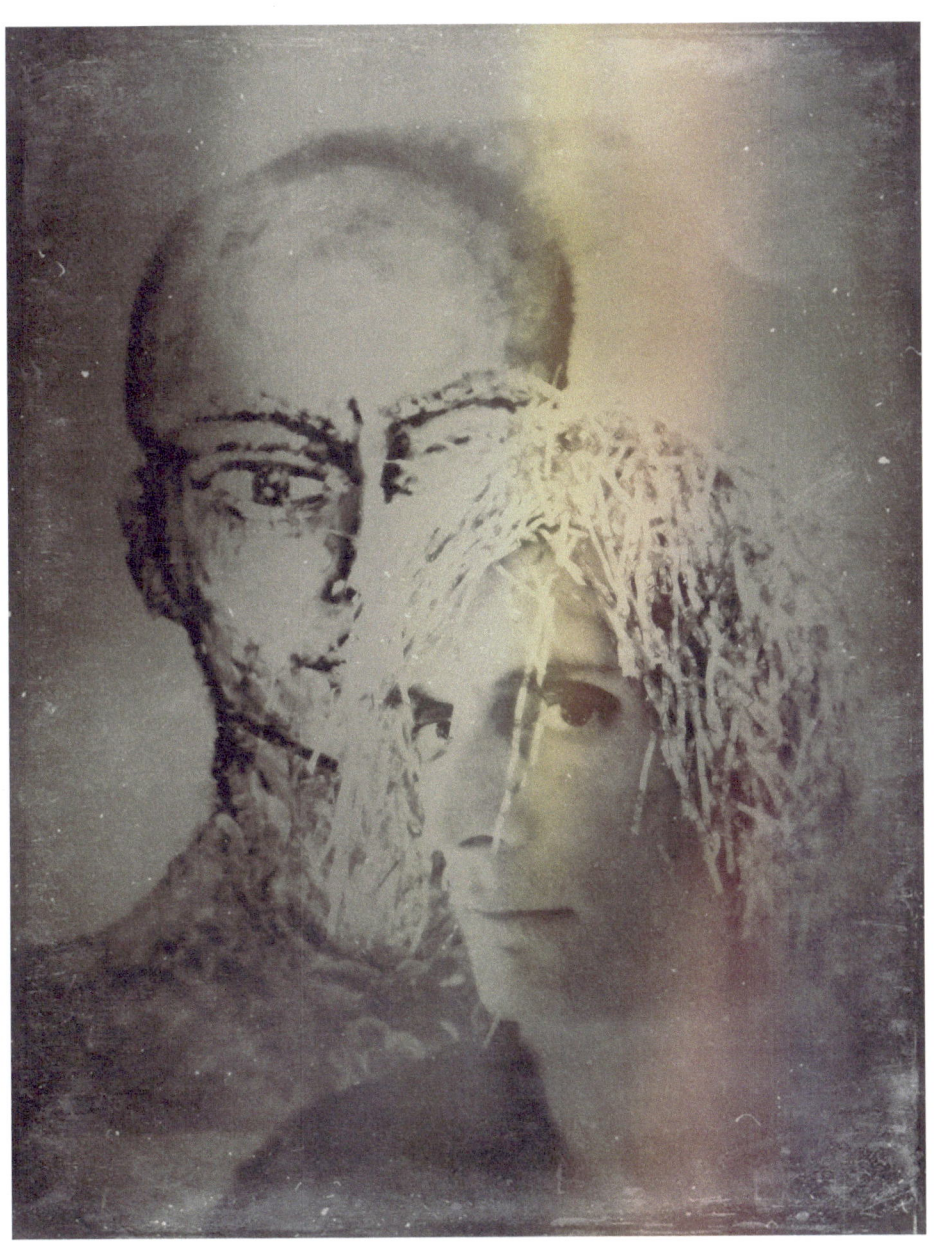

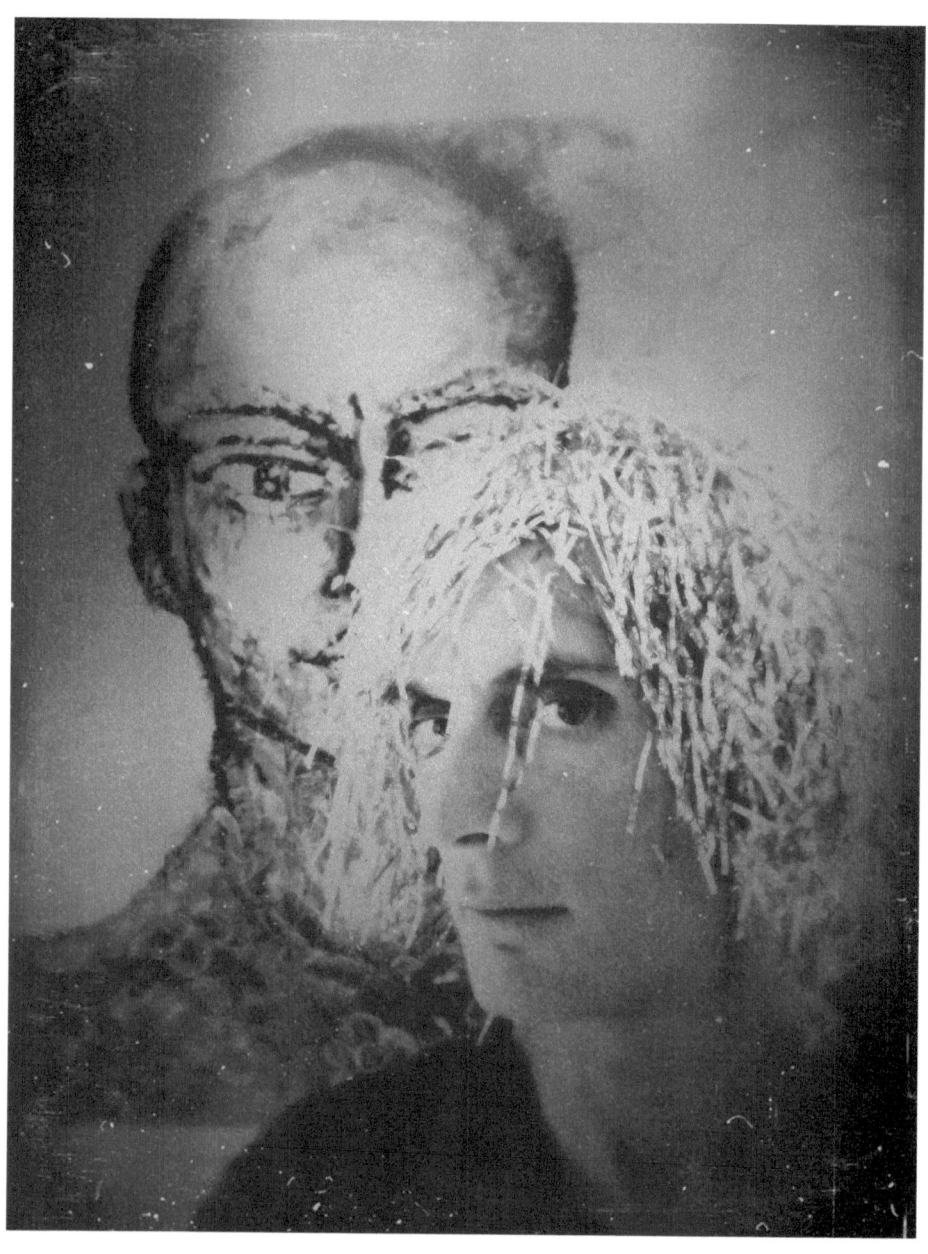

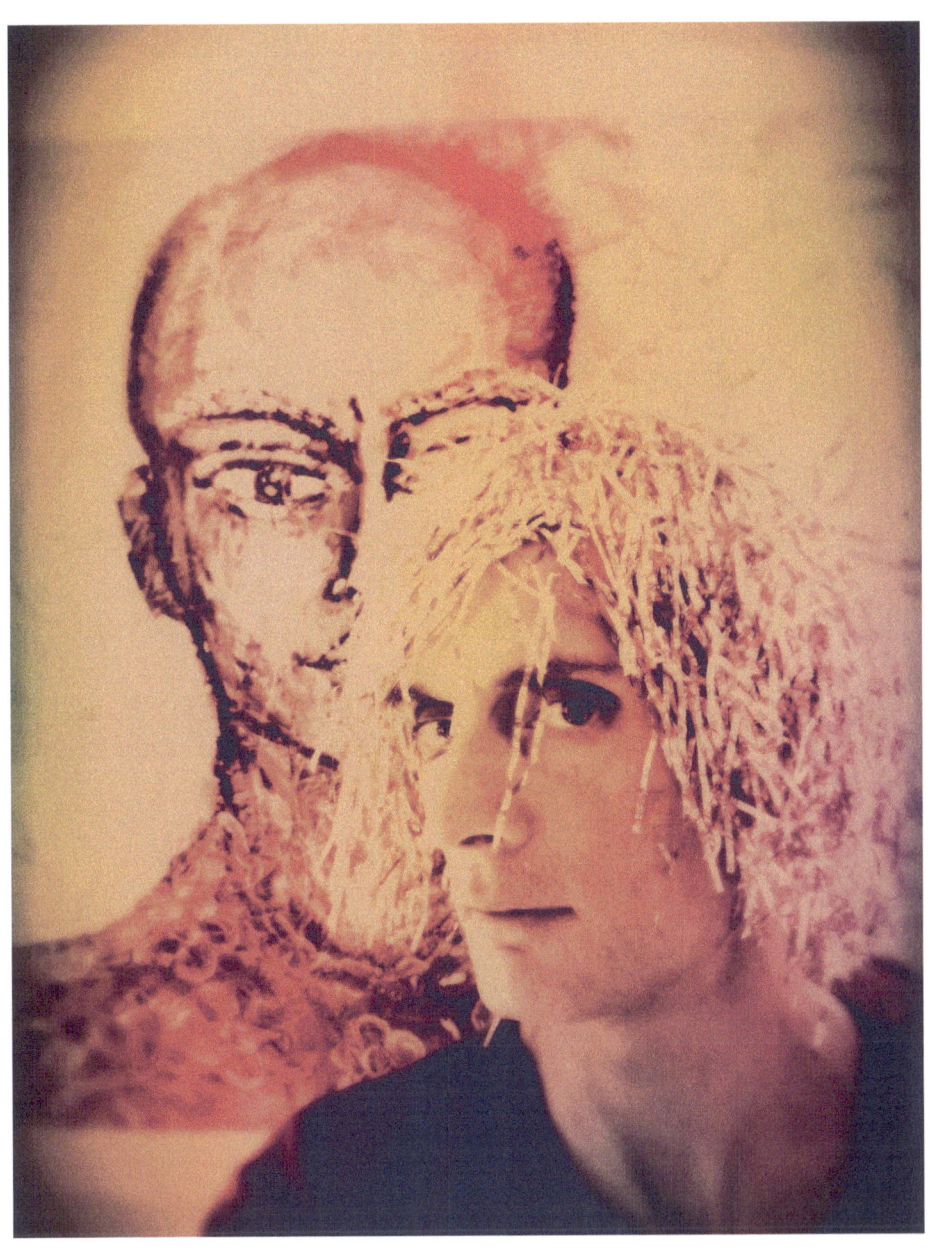

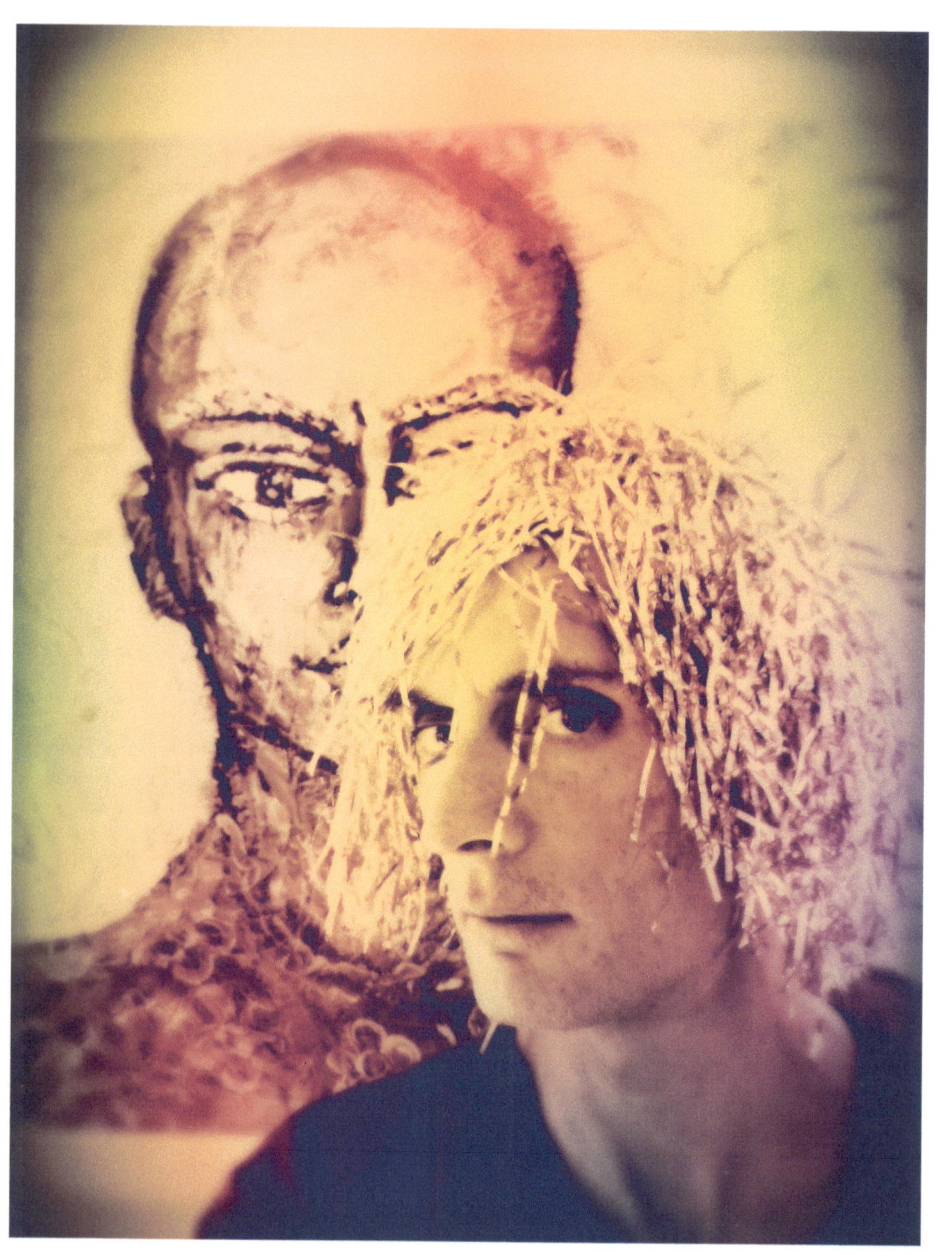

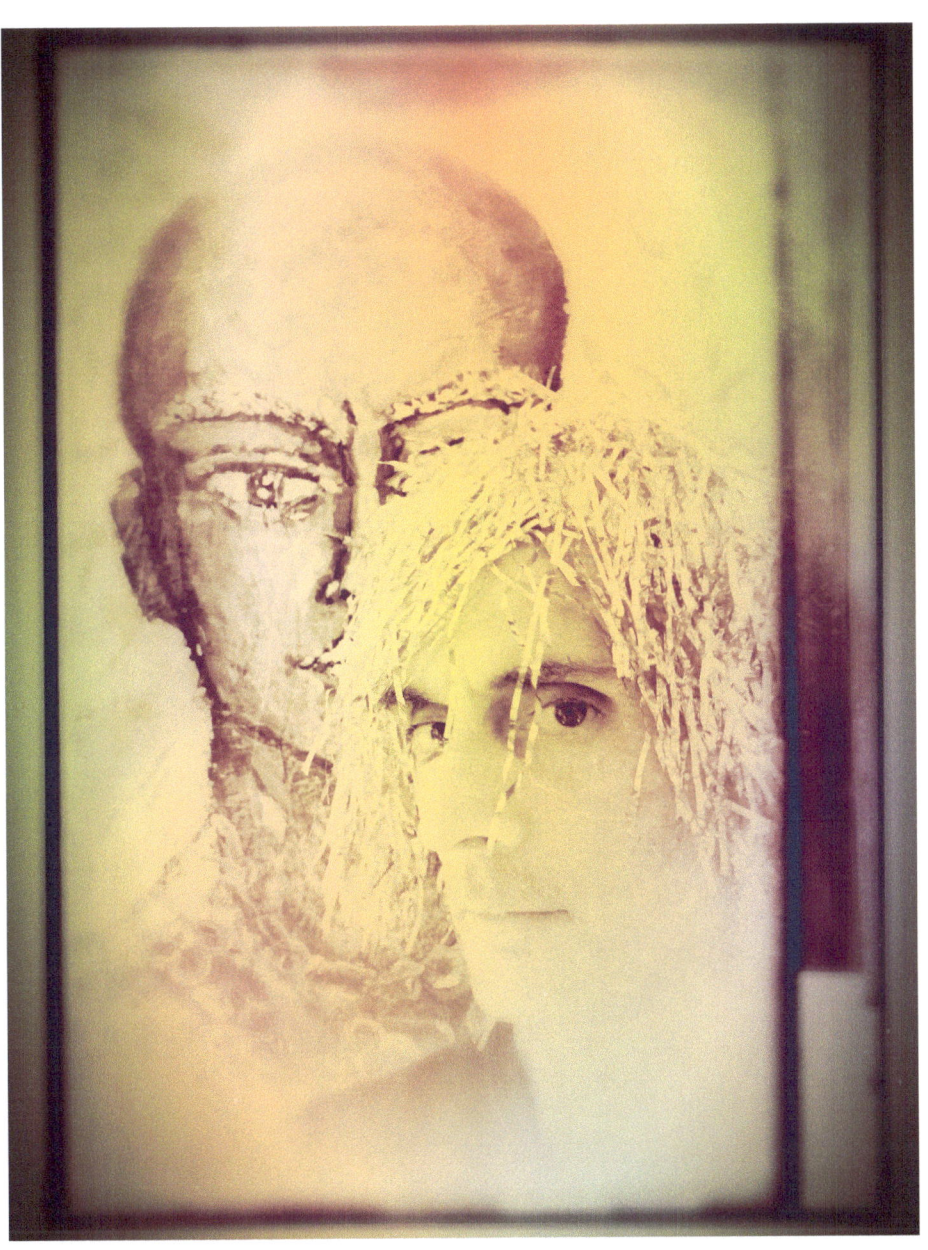

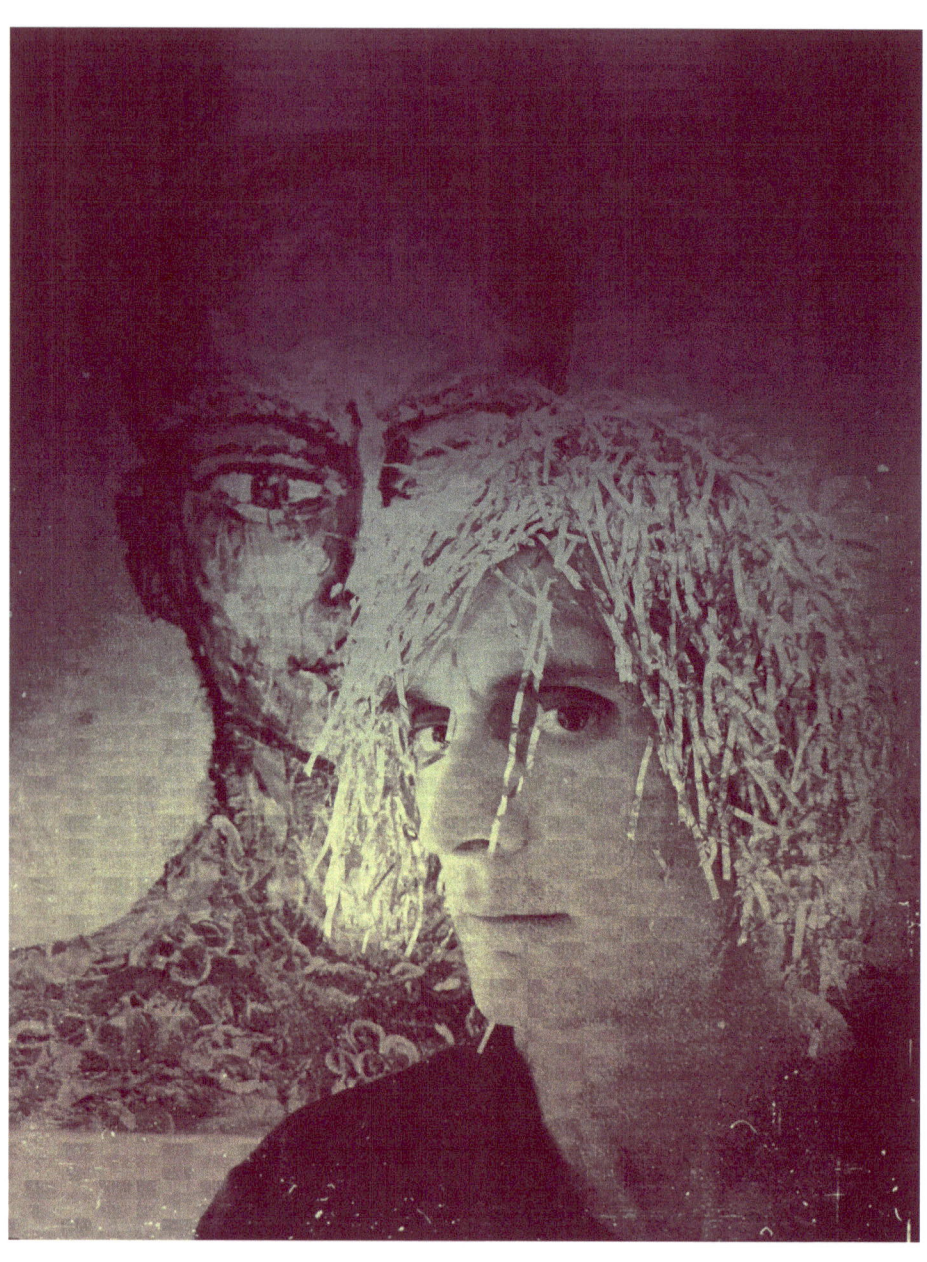

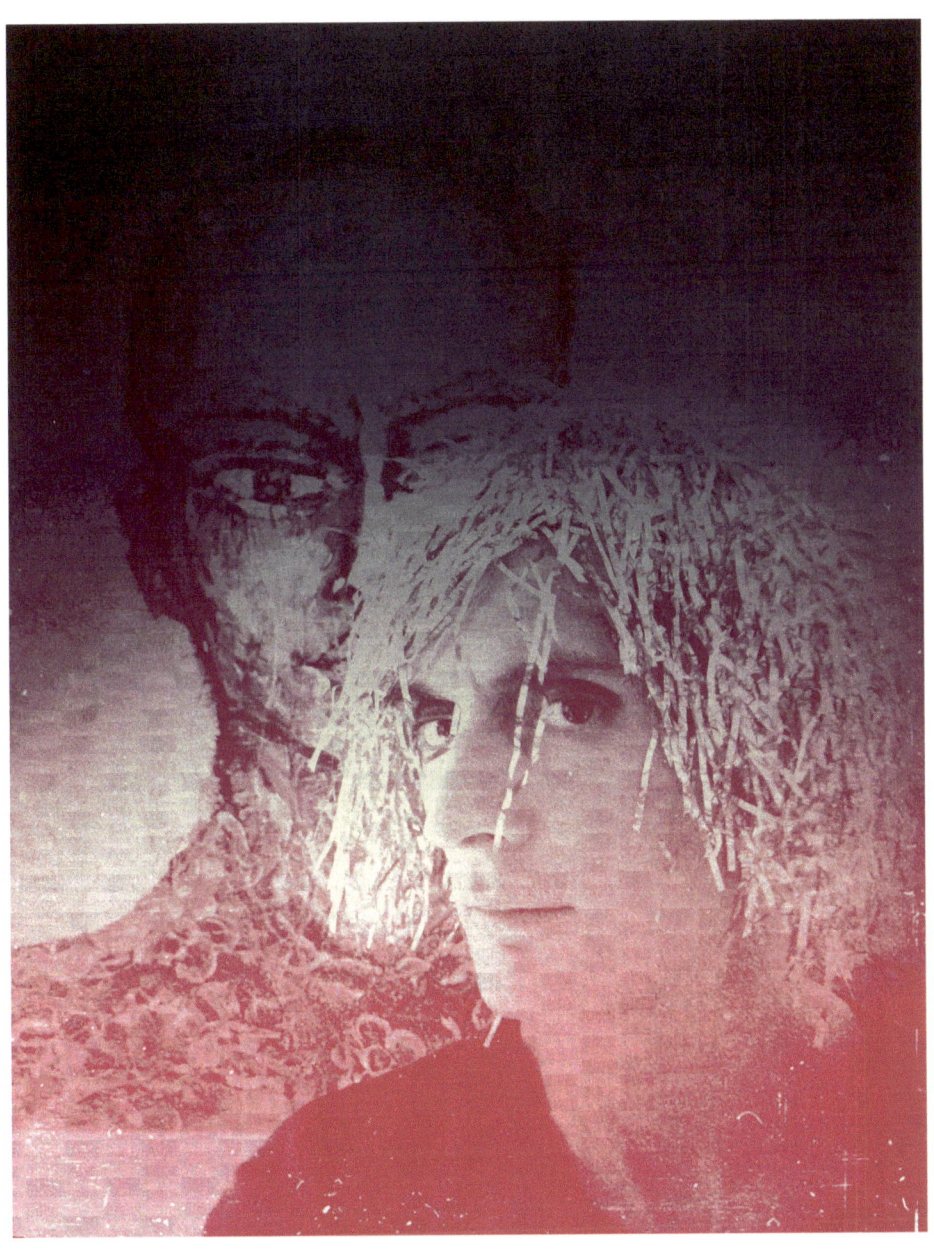

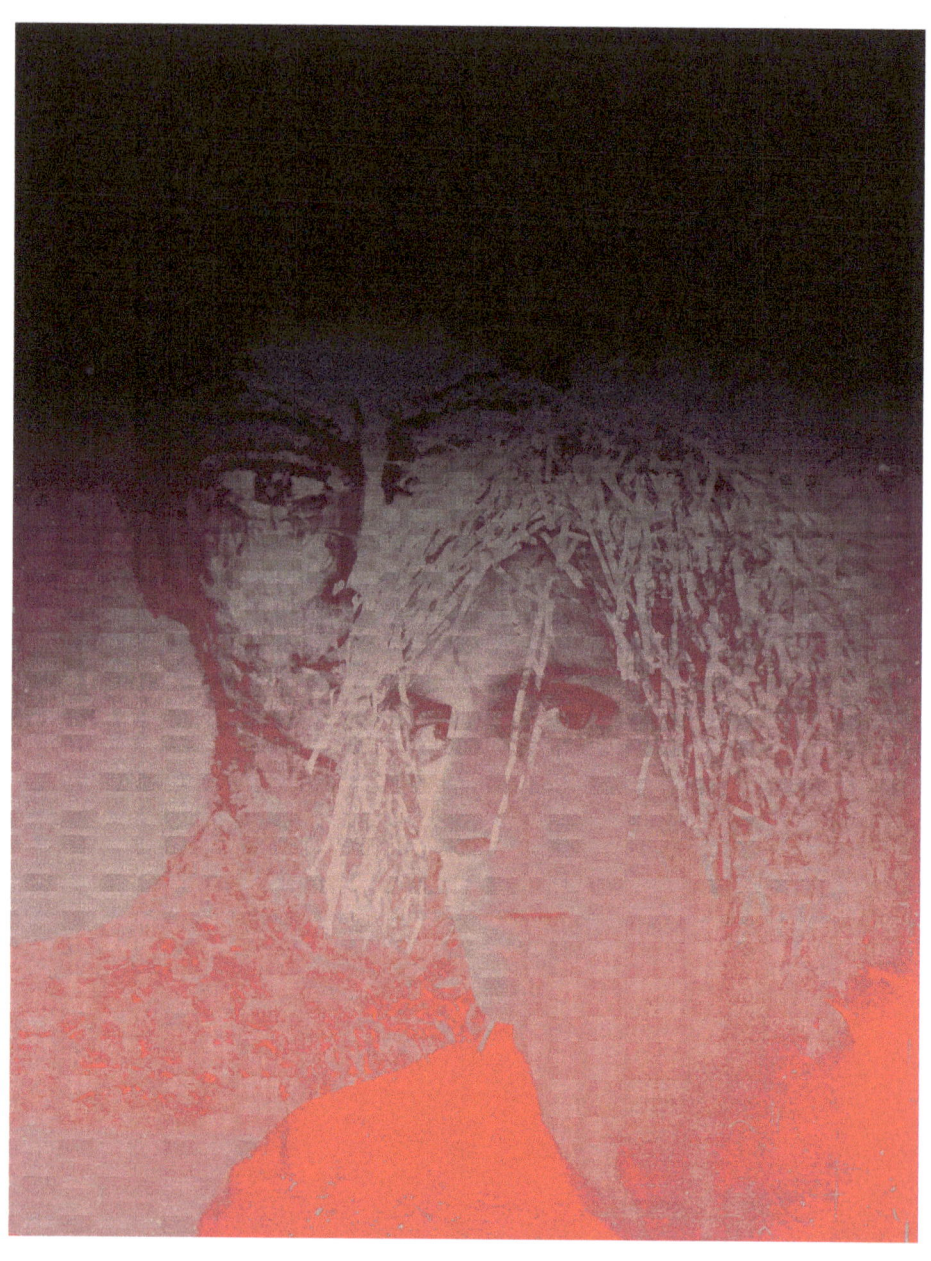

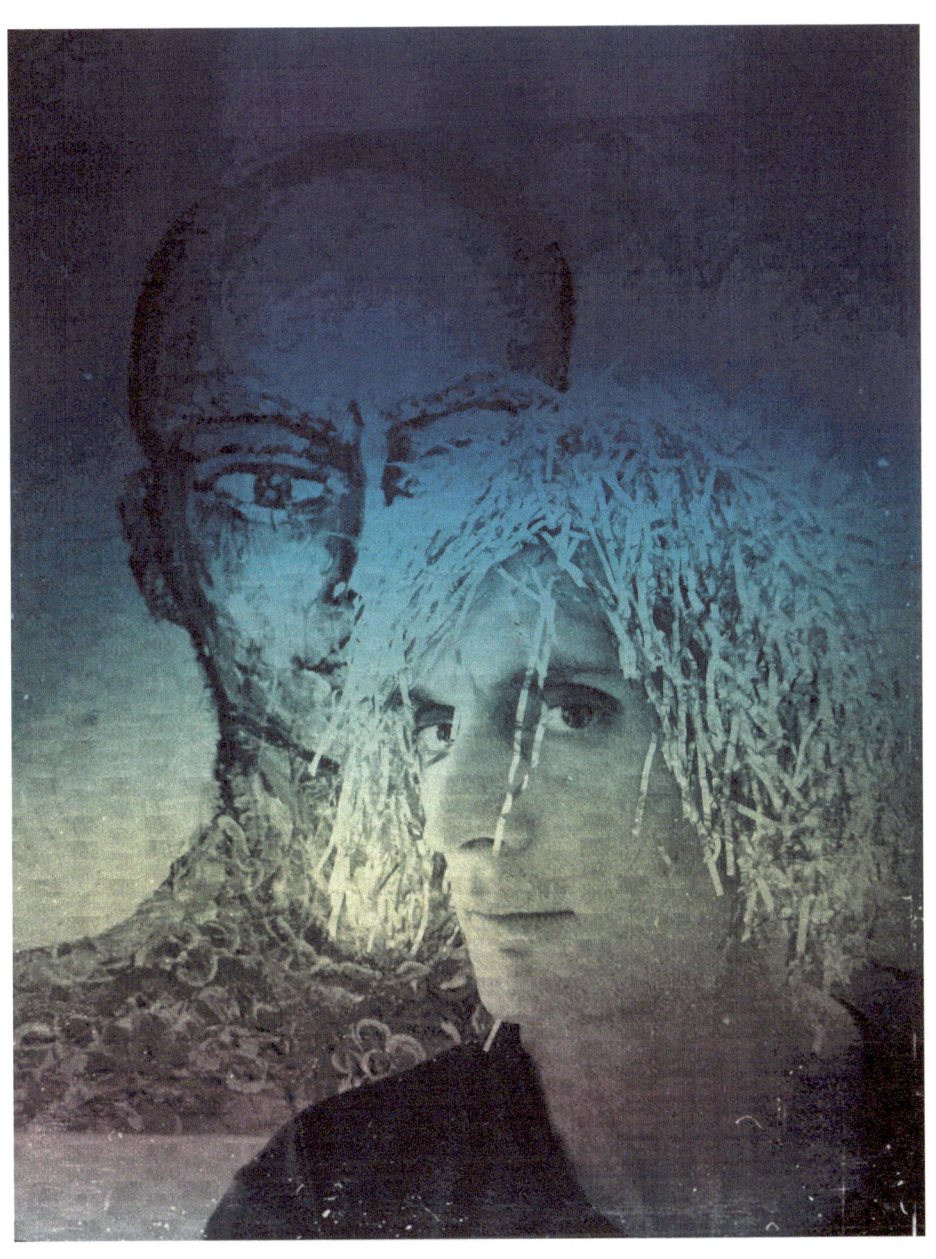

11

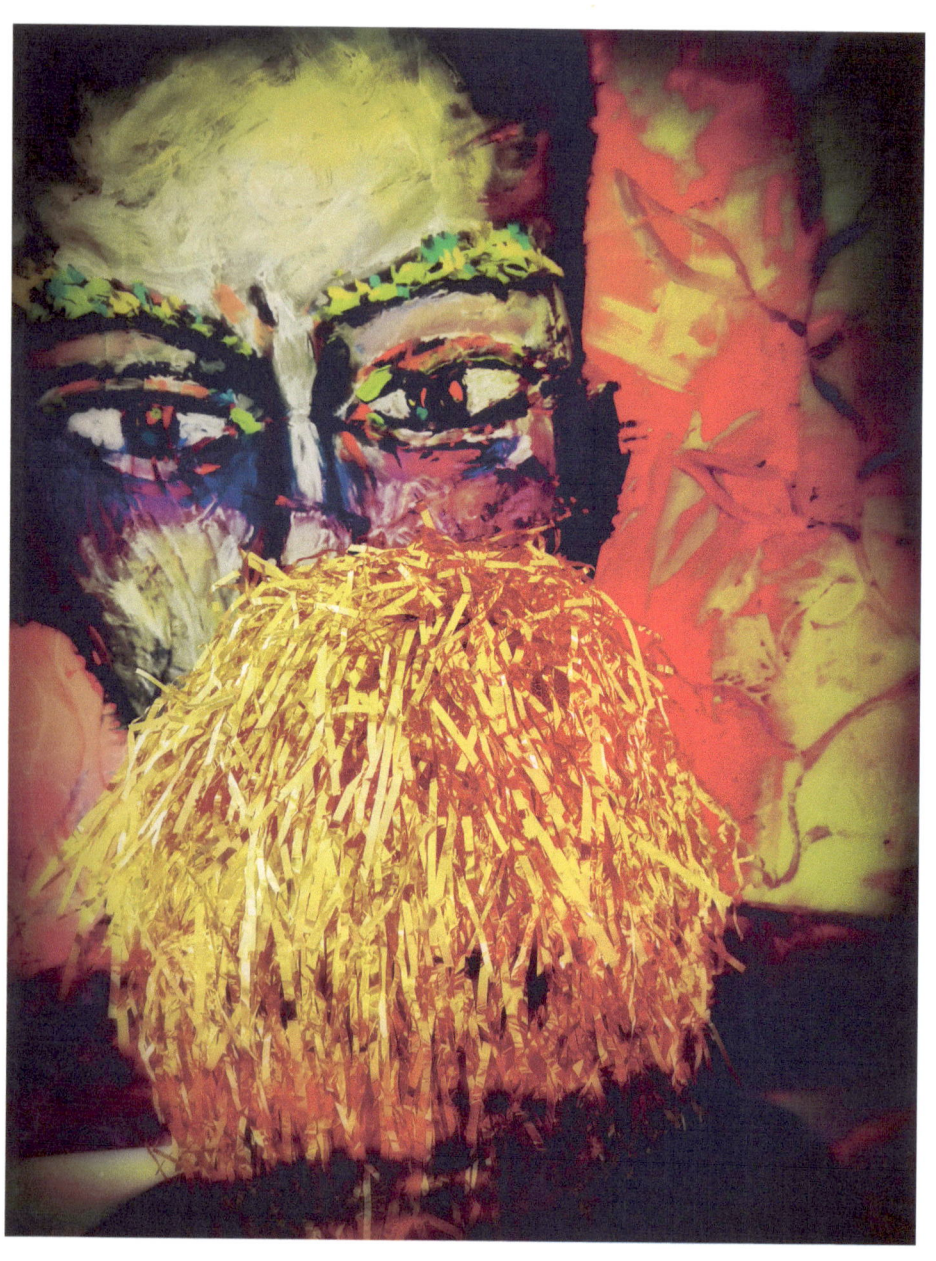

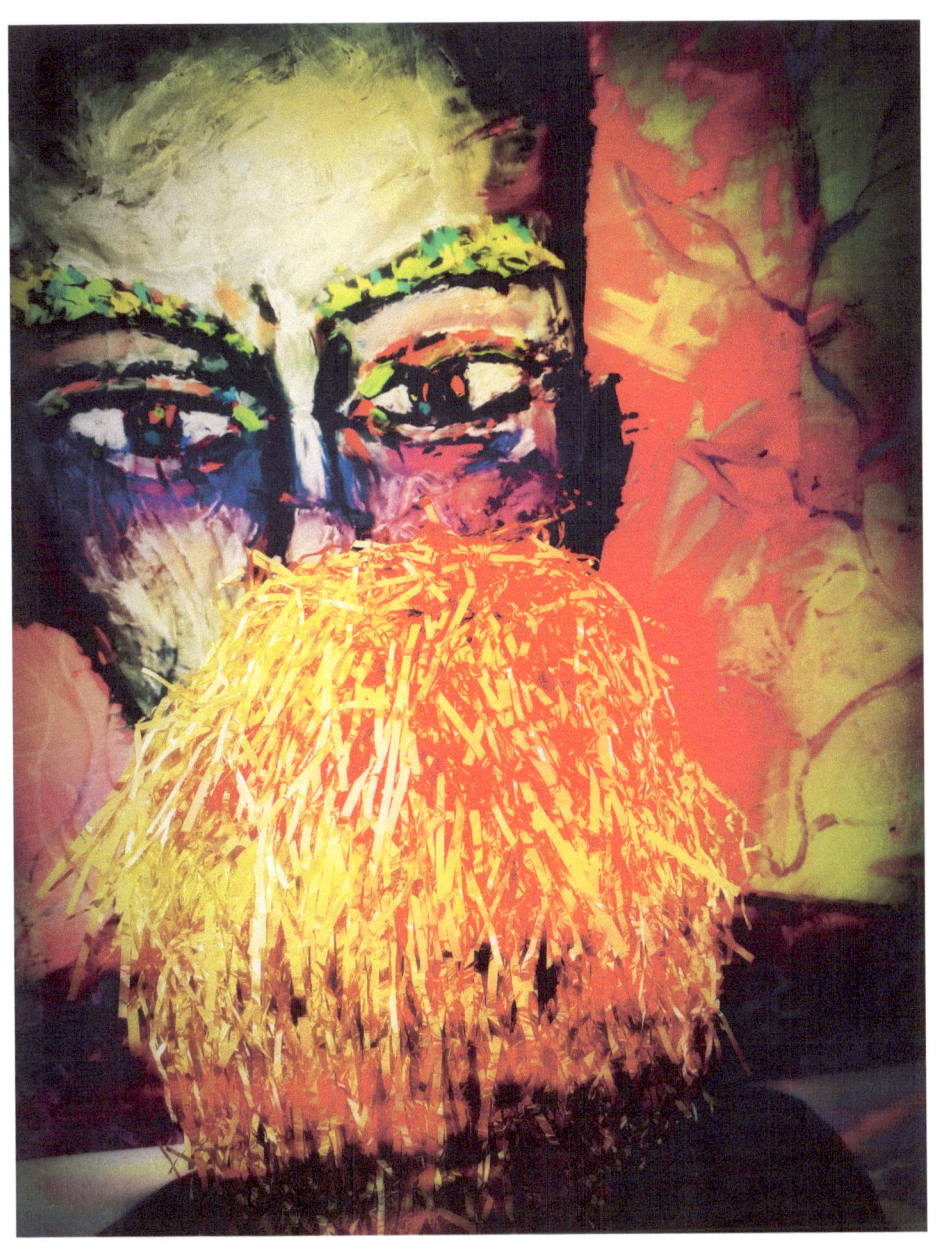

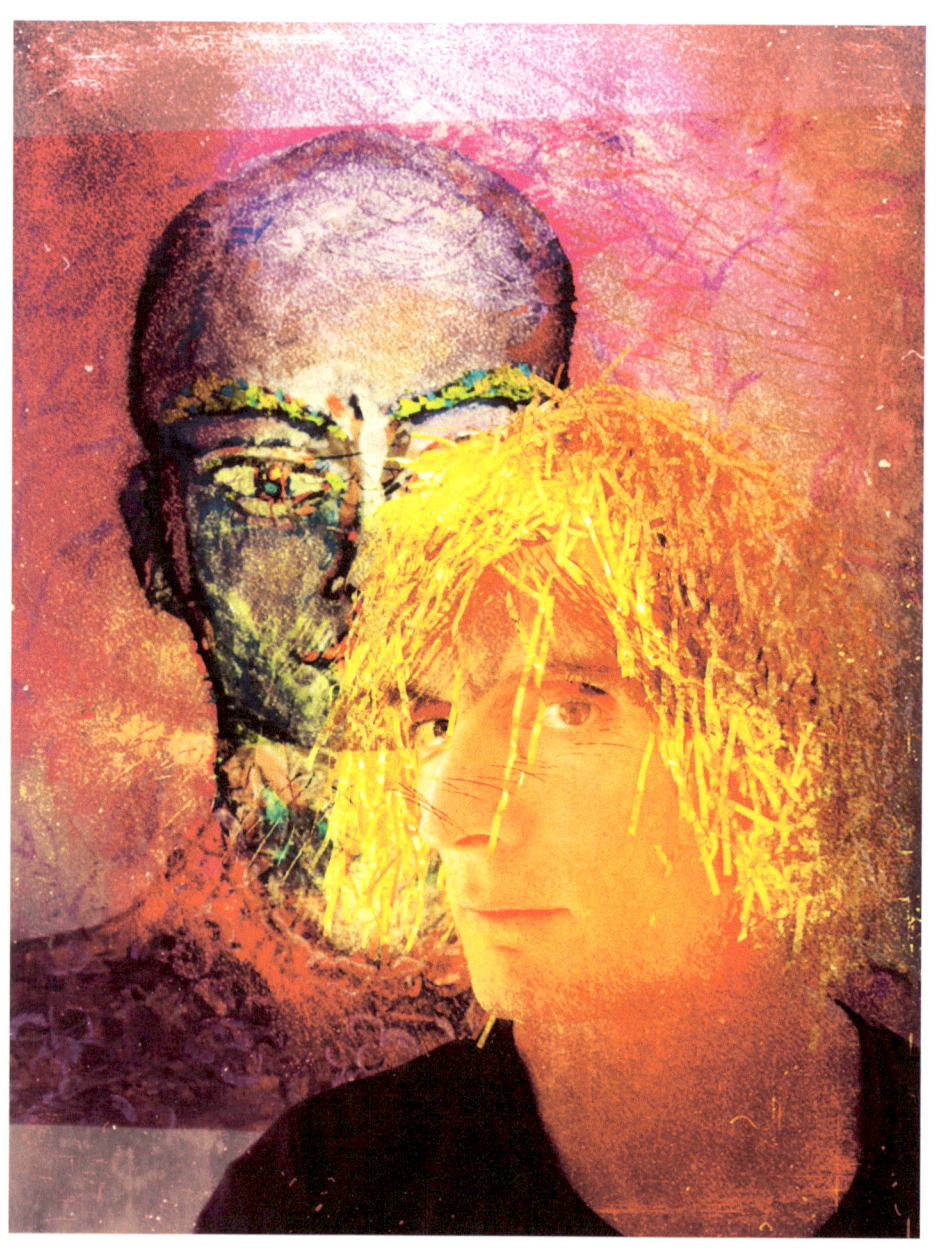

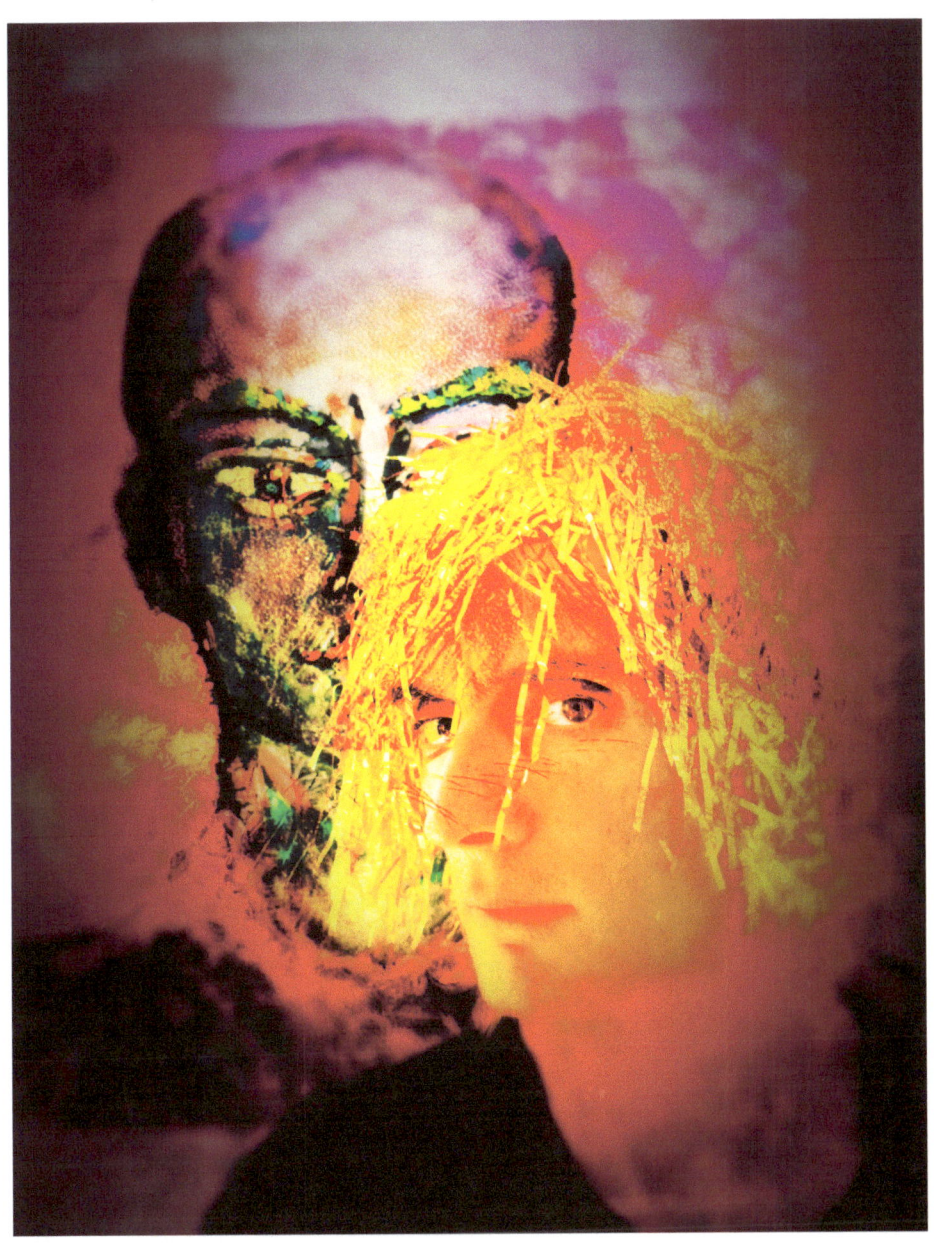

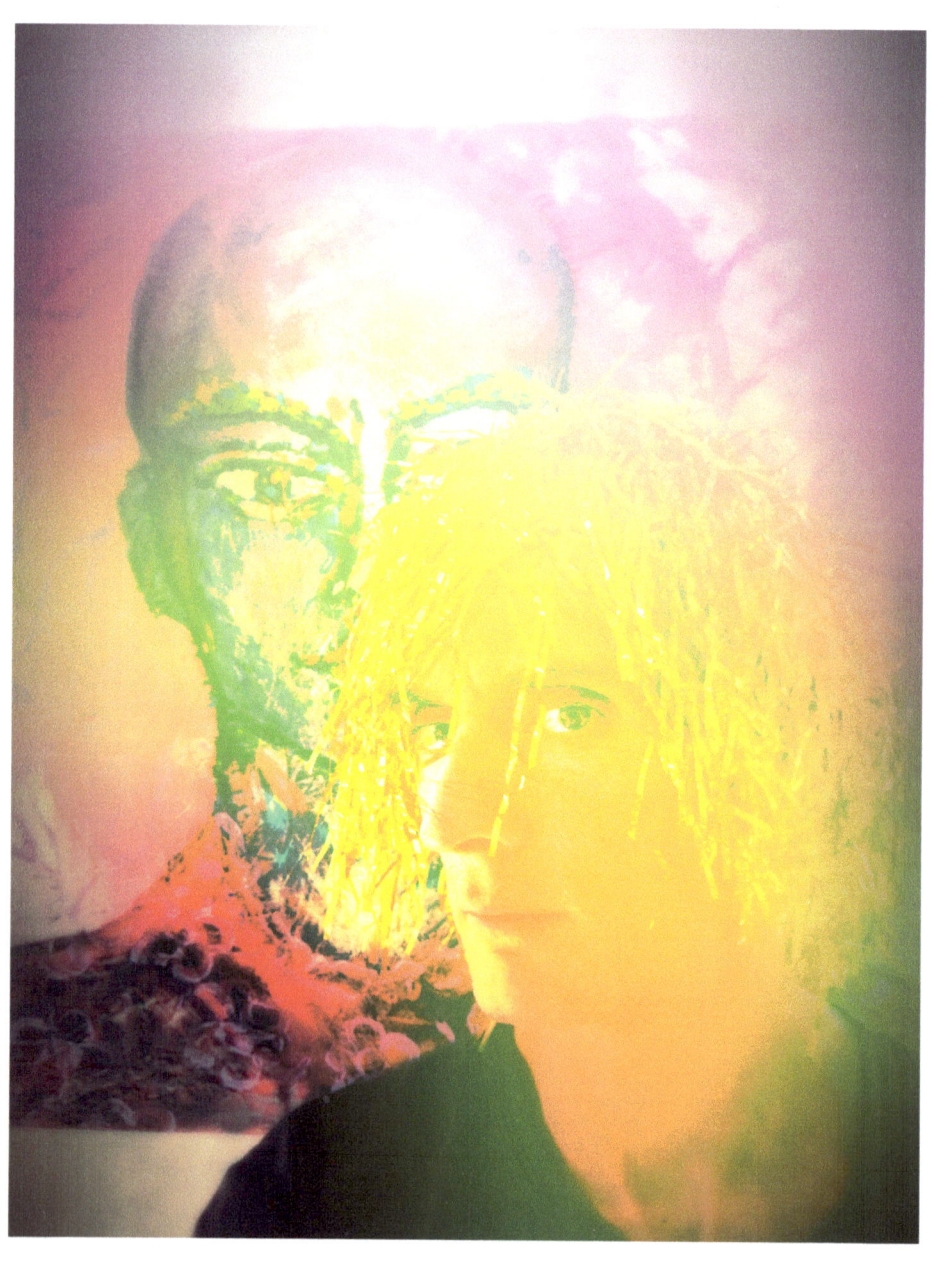

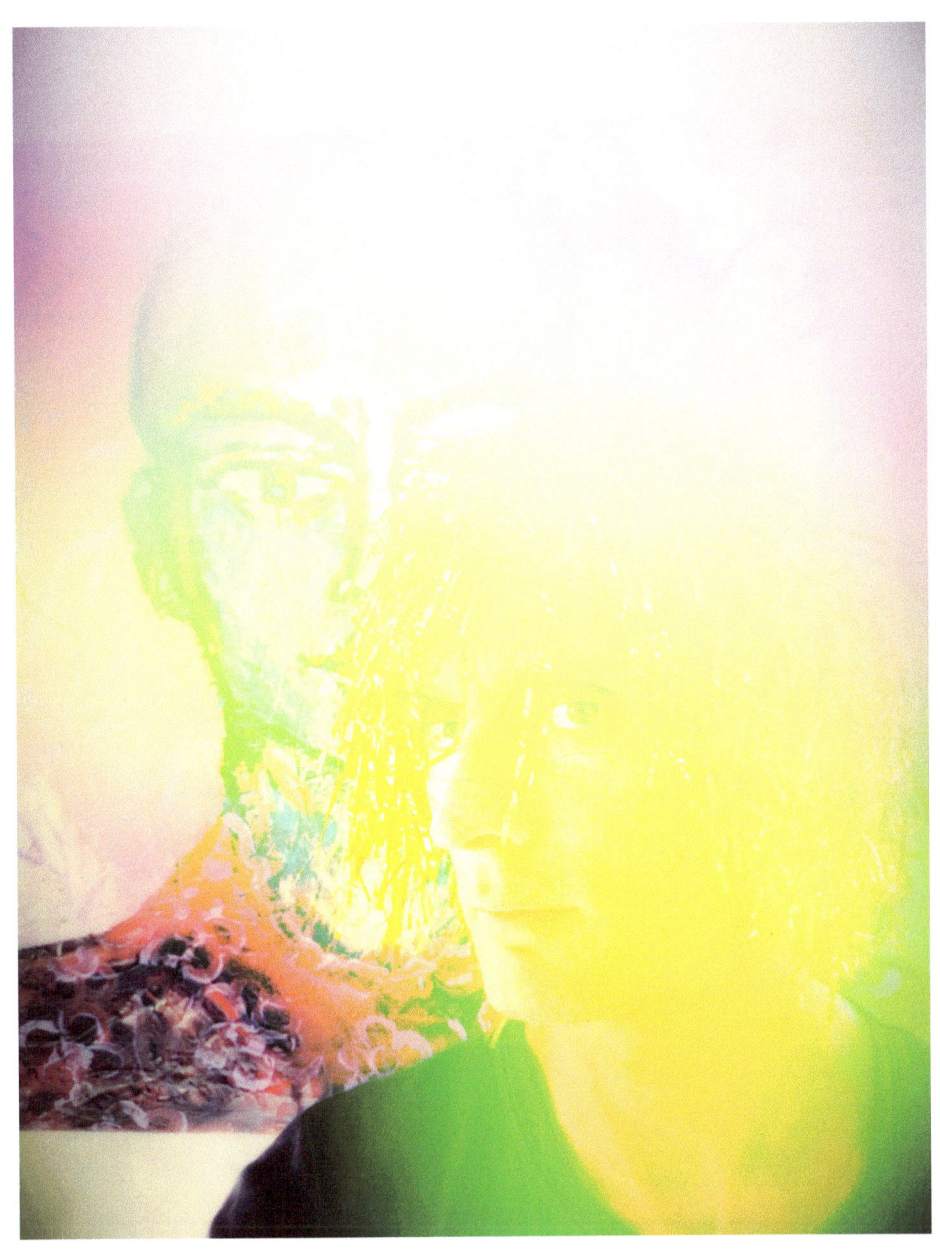

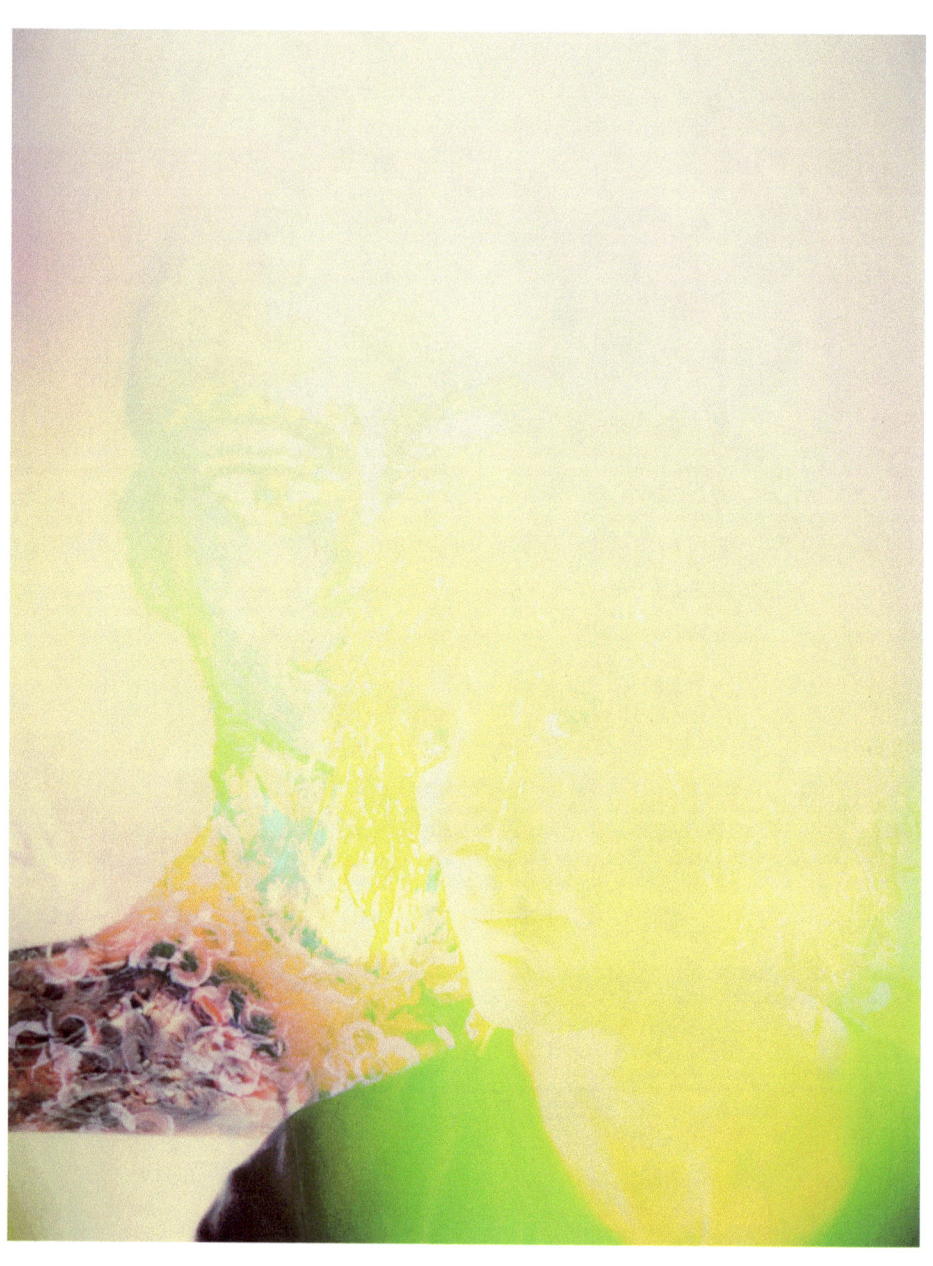

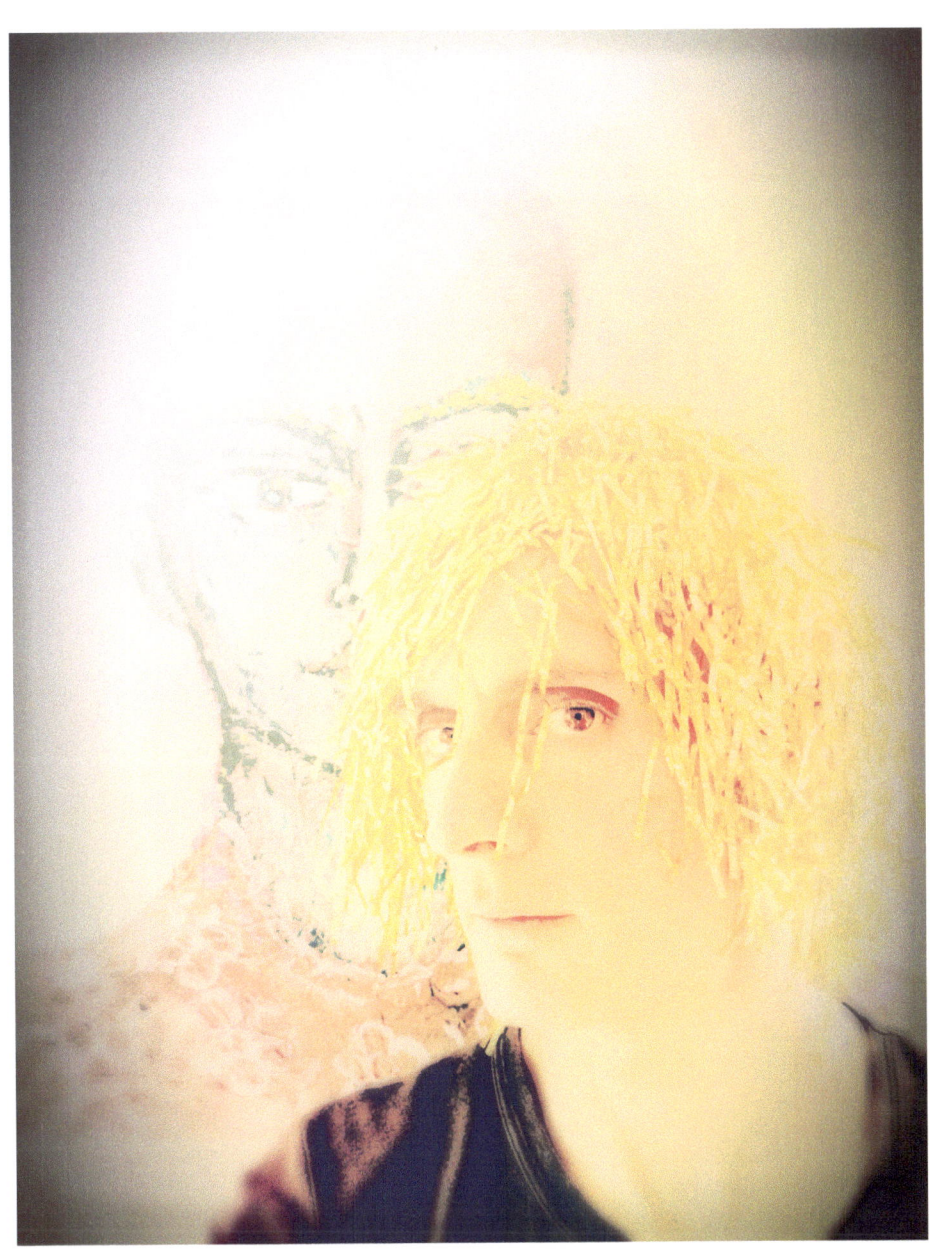

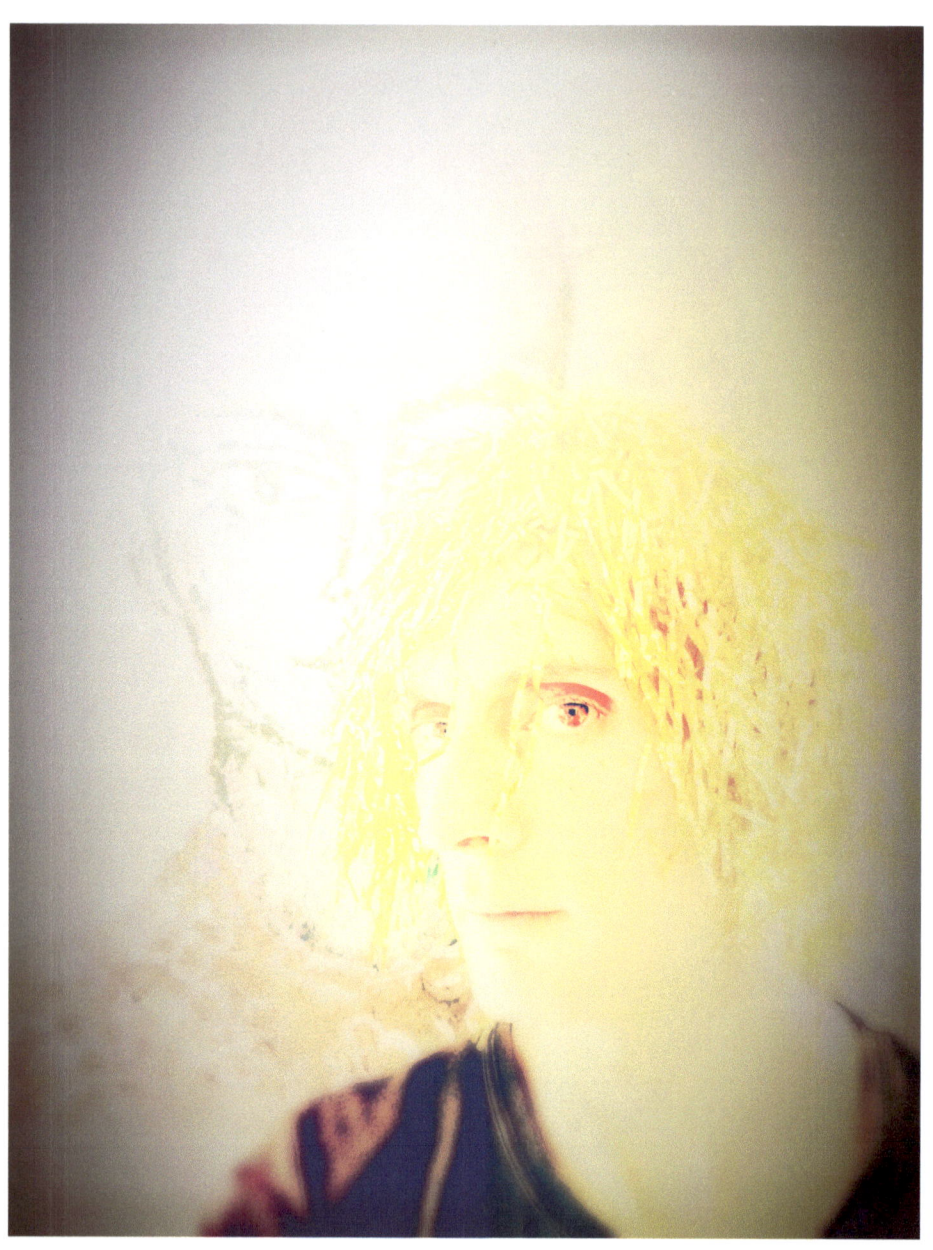

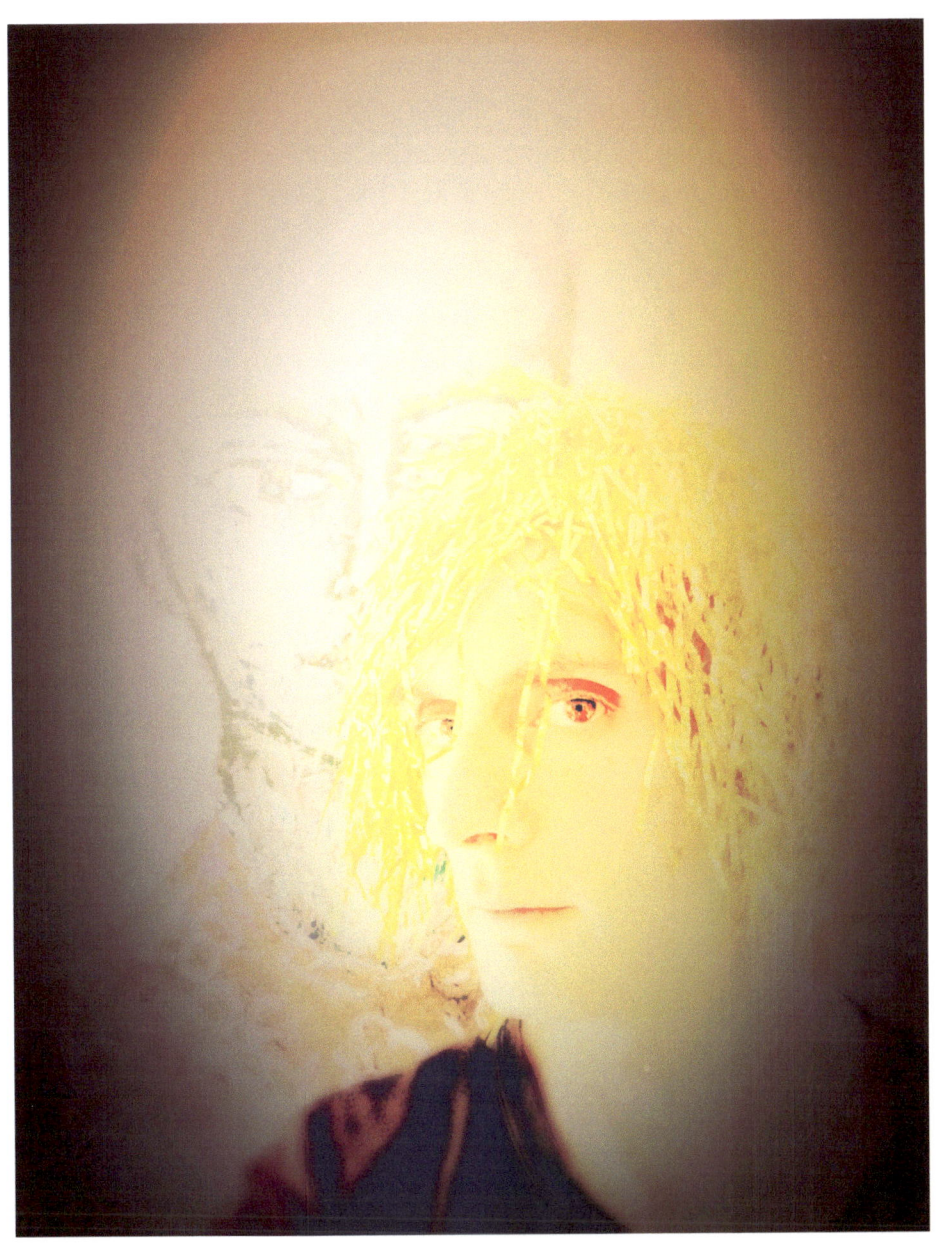

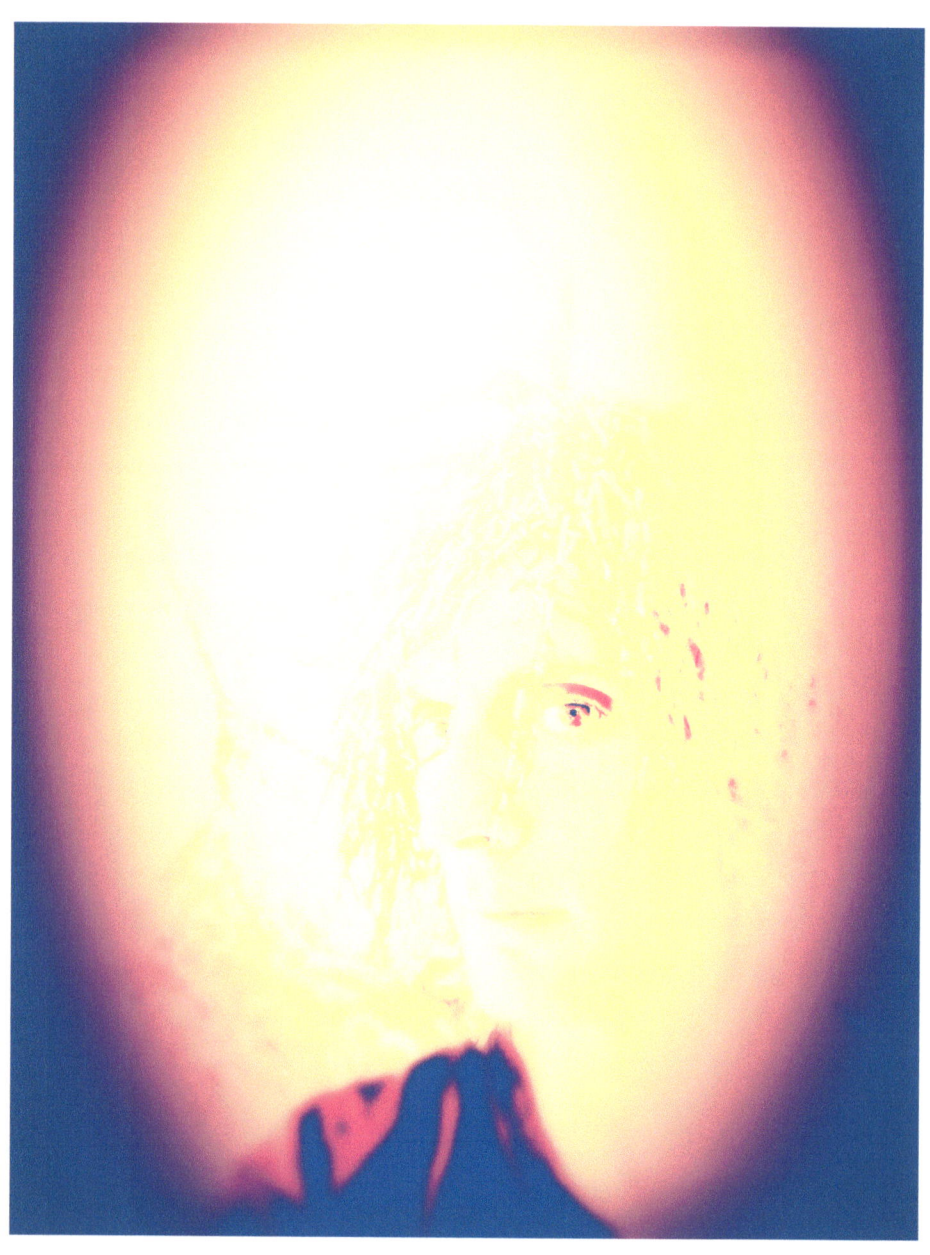

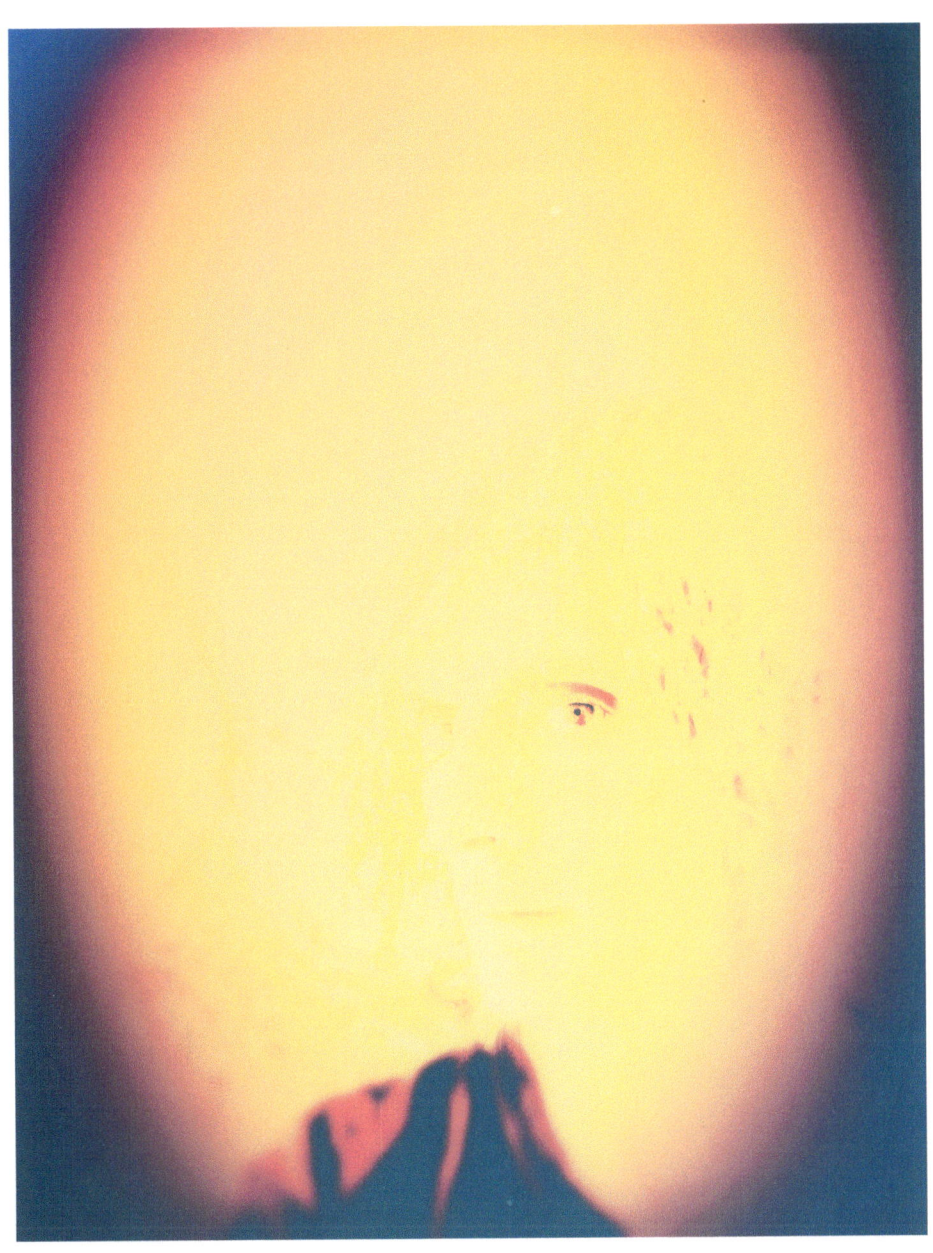

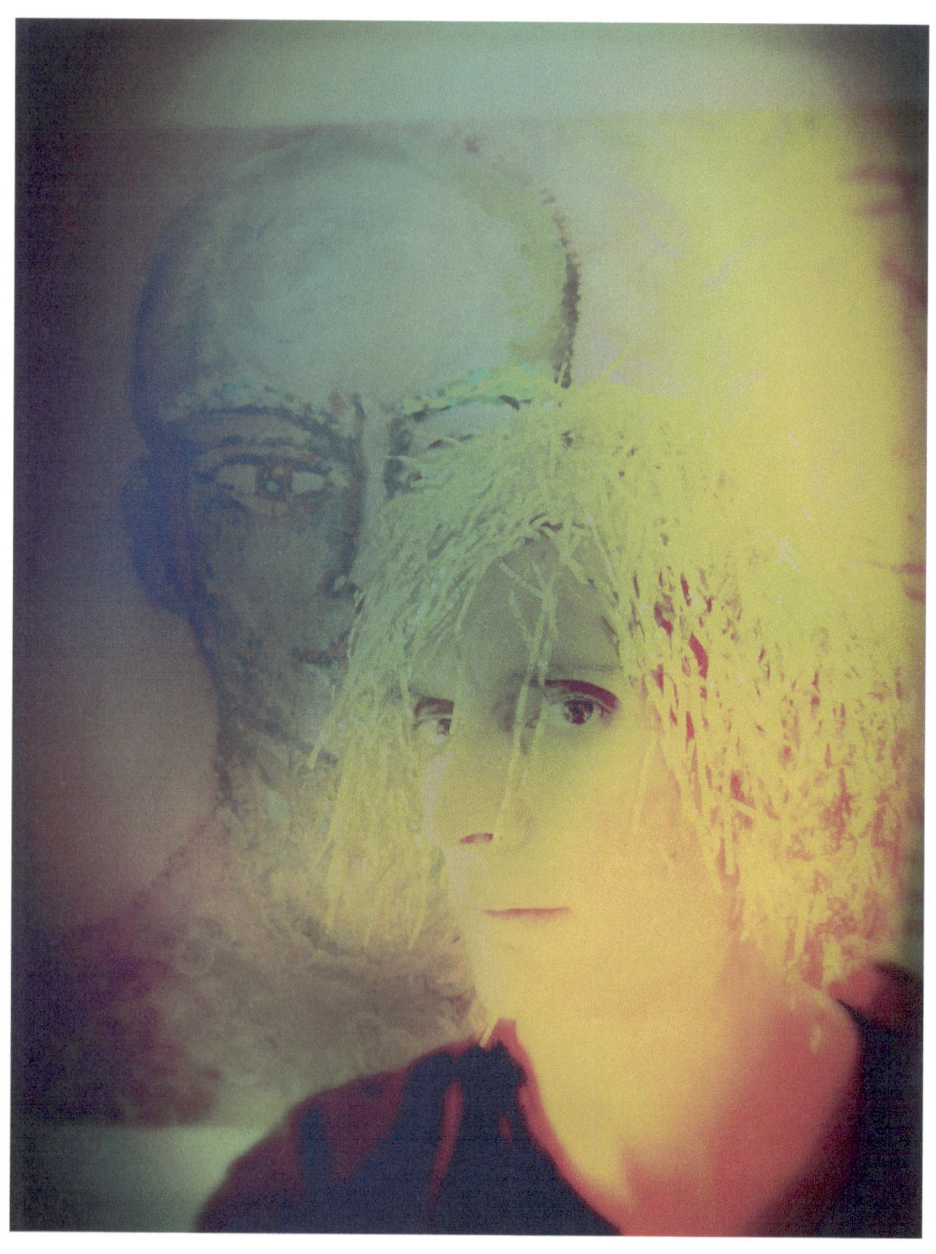

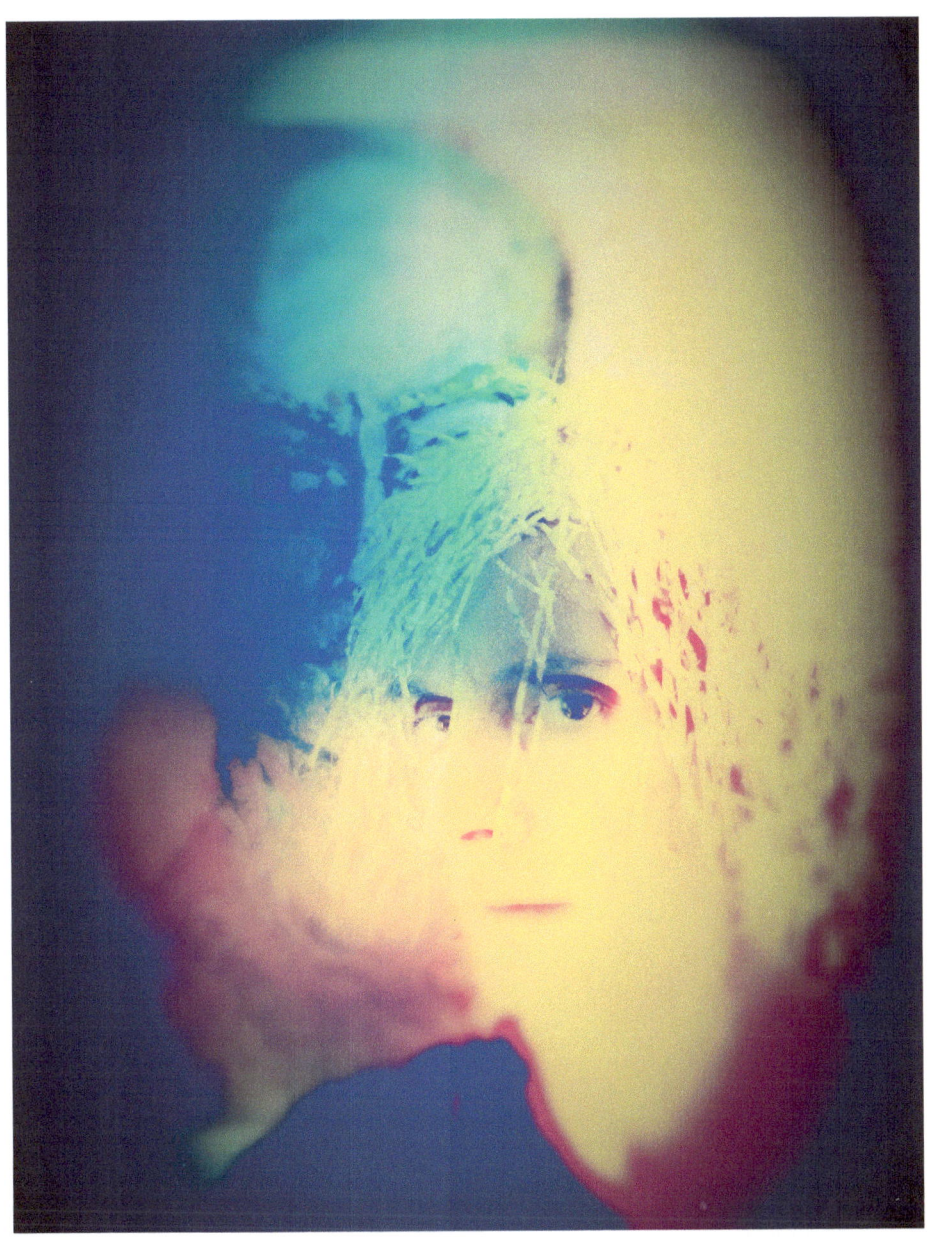

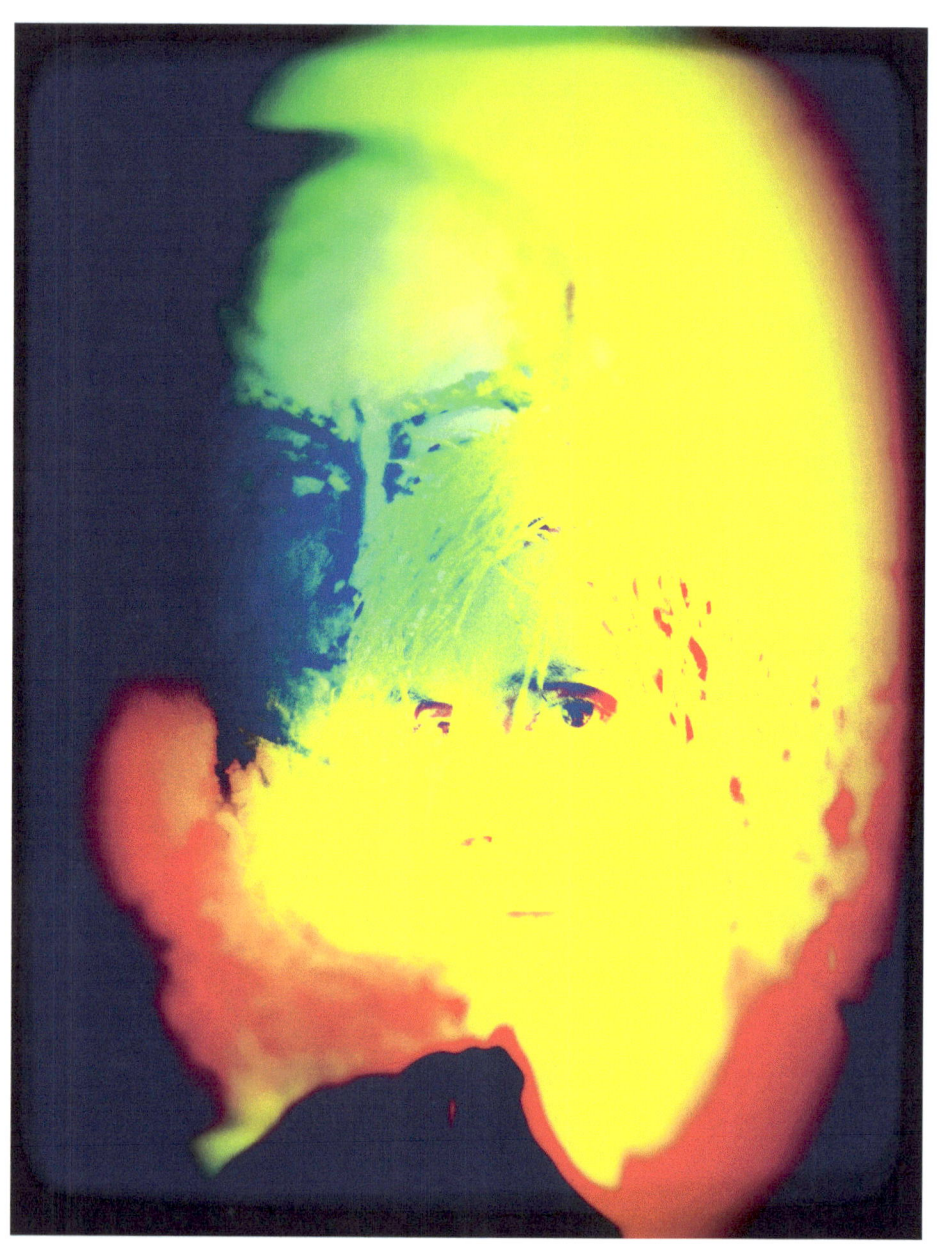

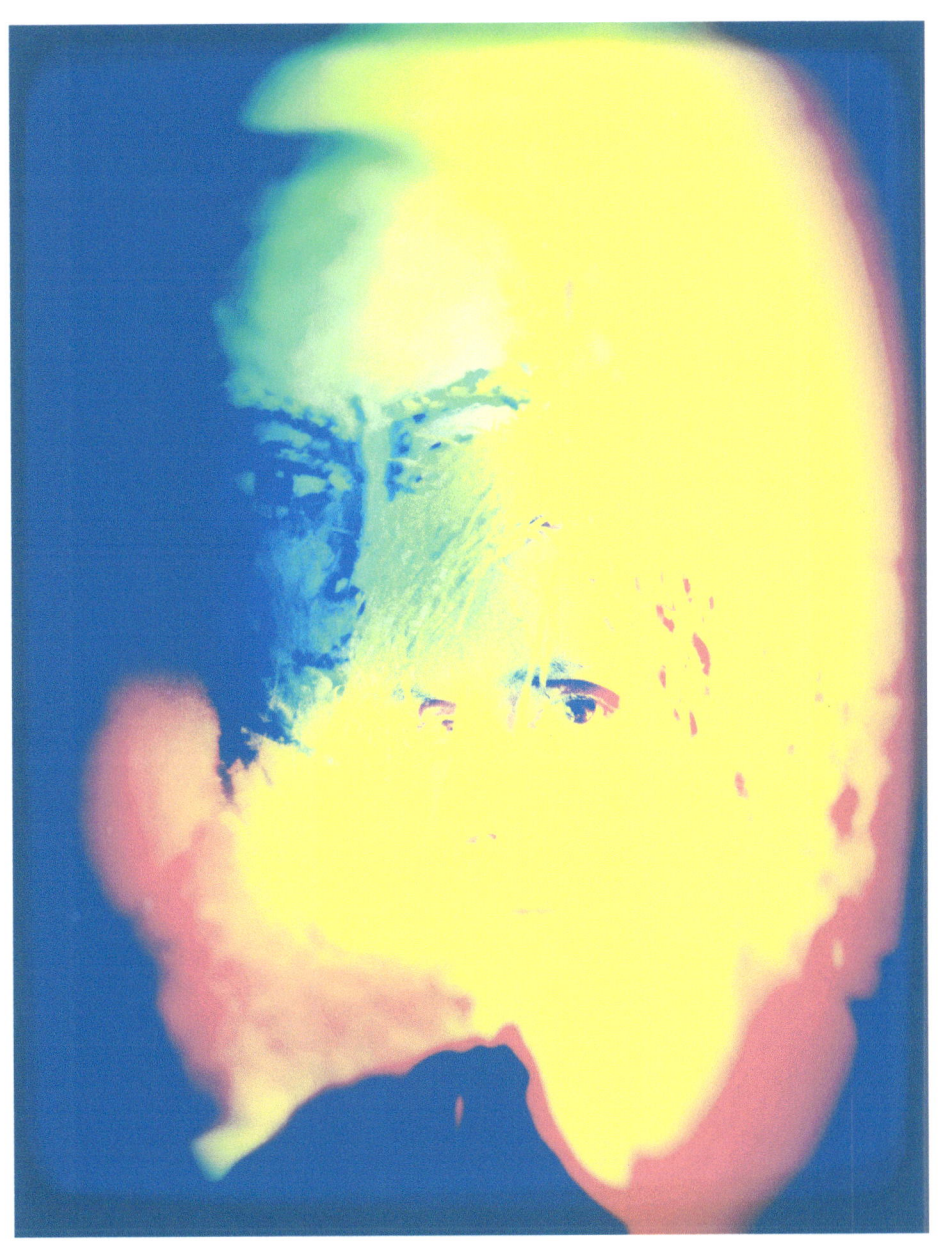

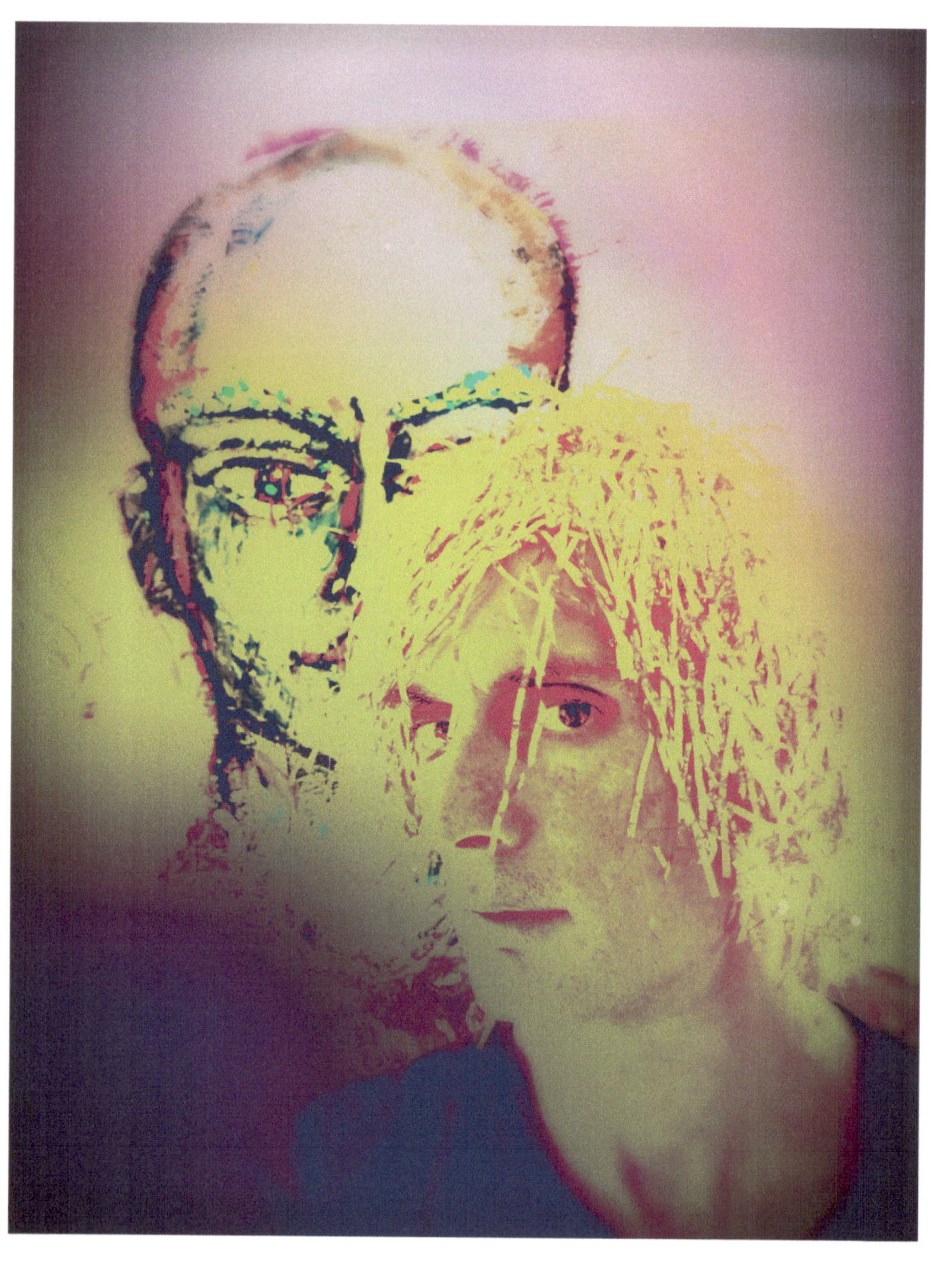

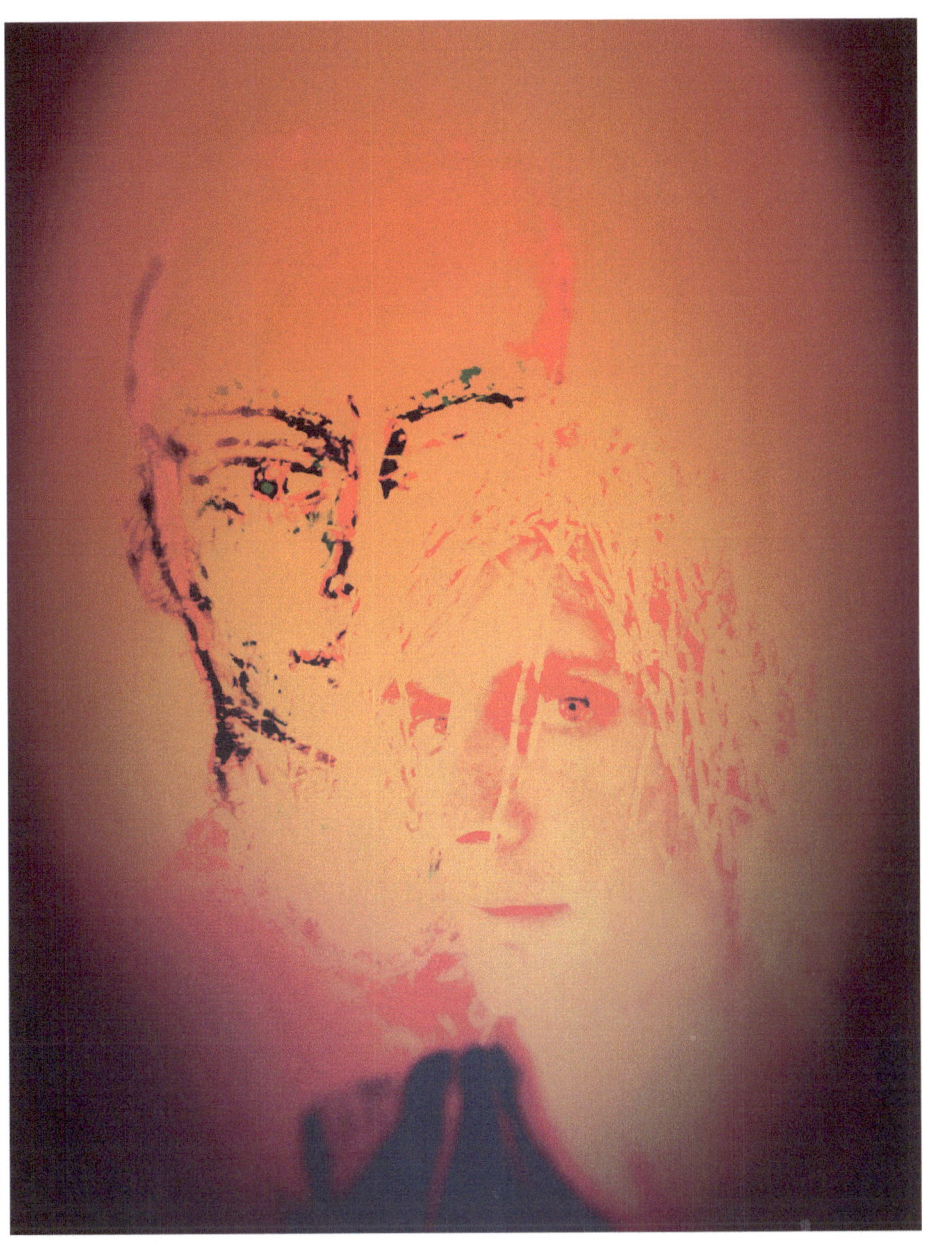

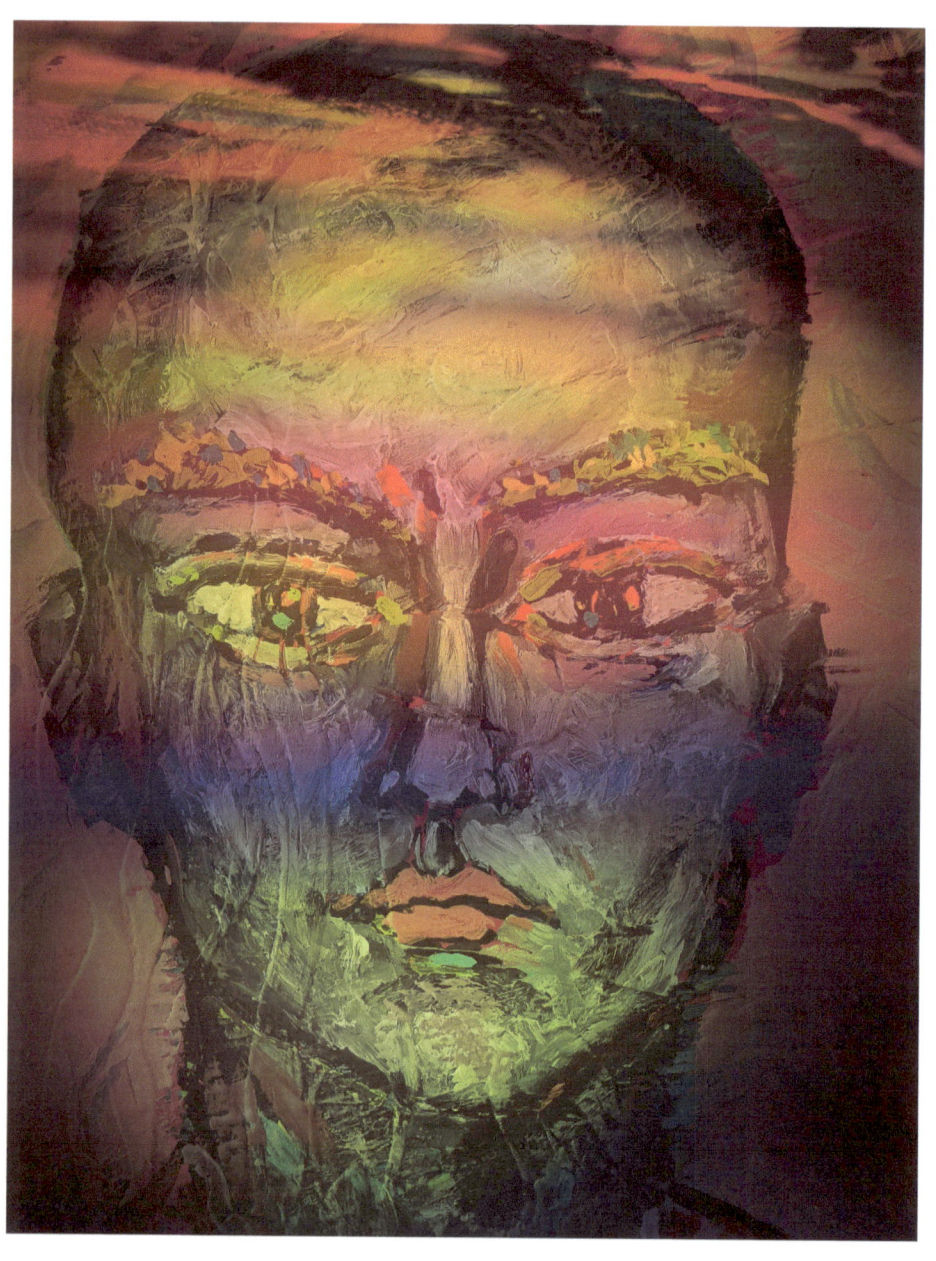

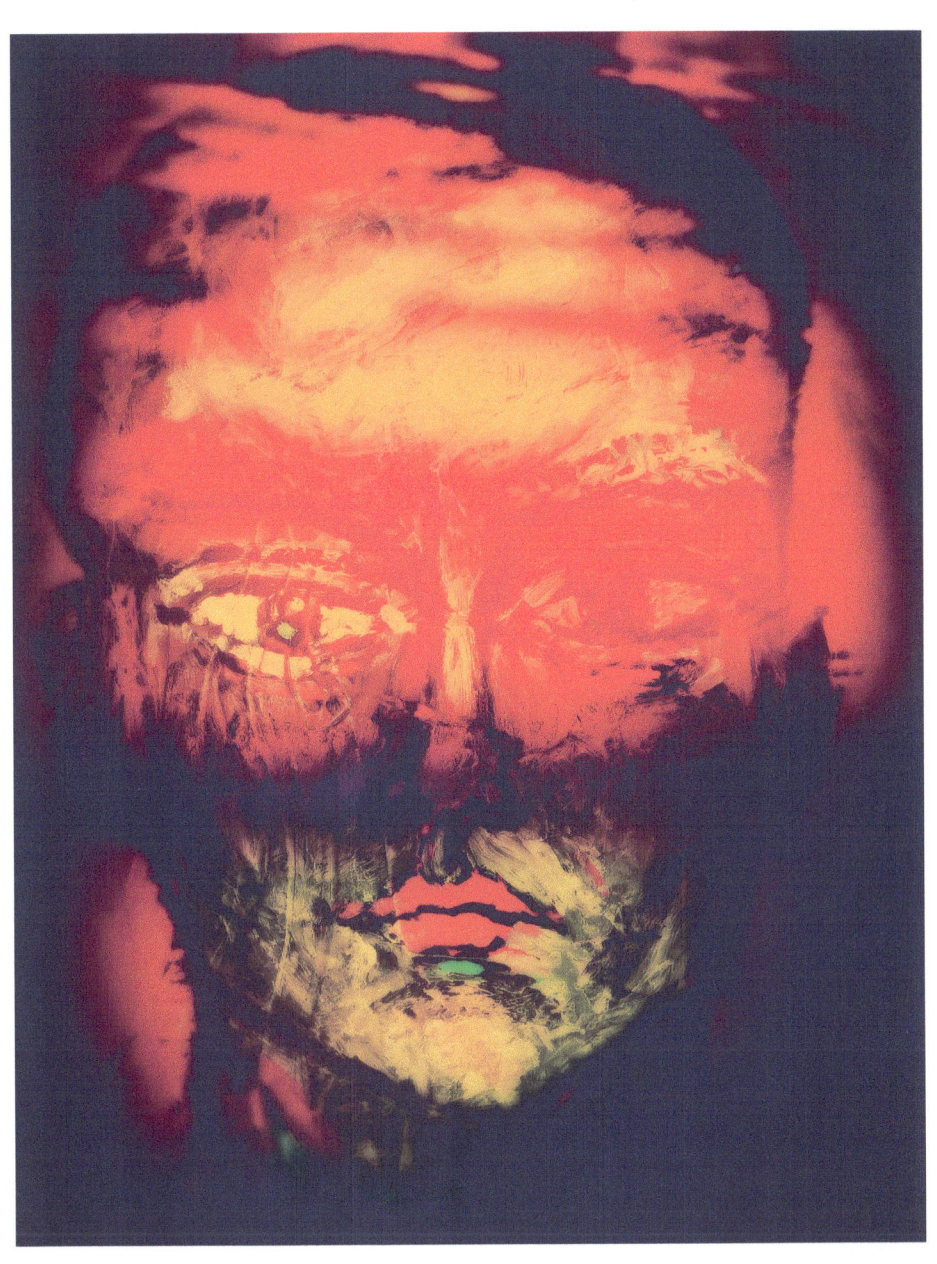

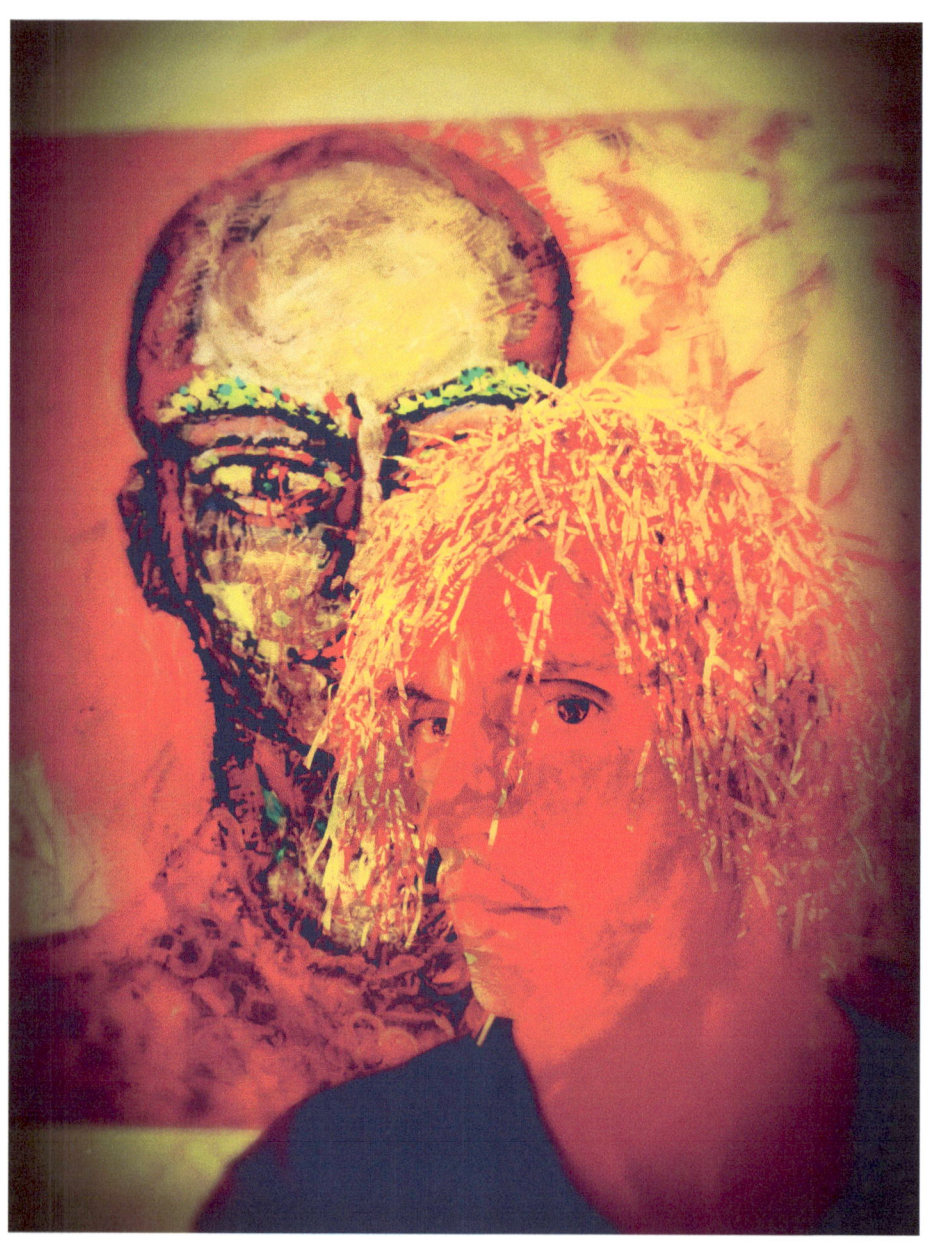

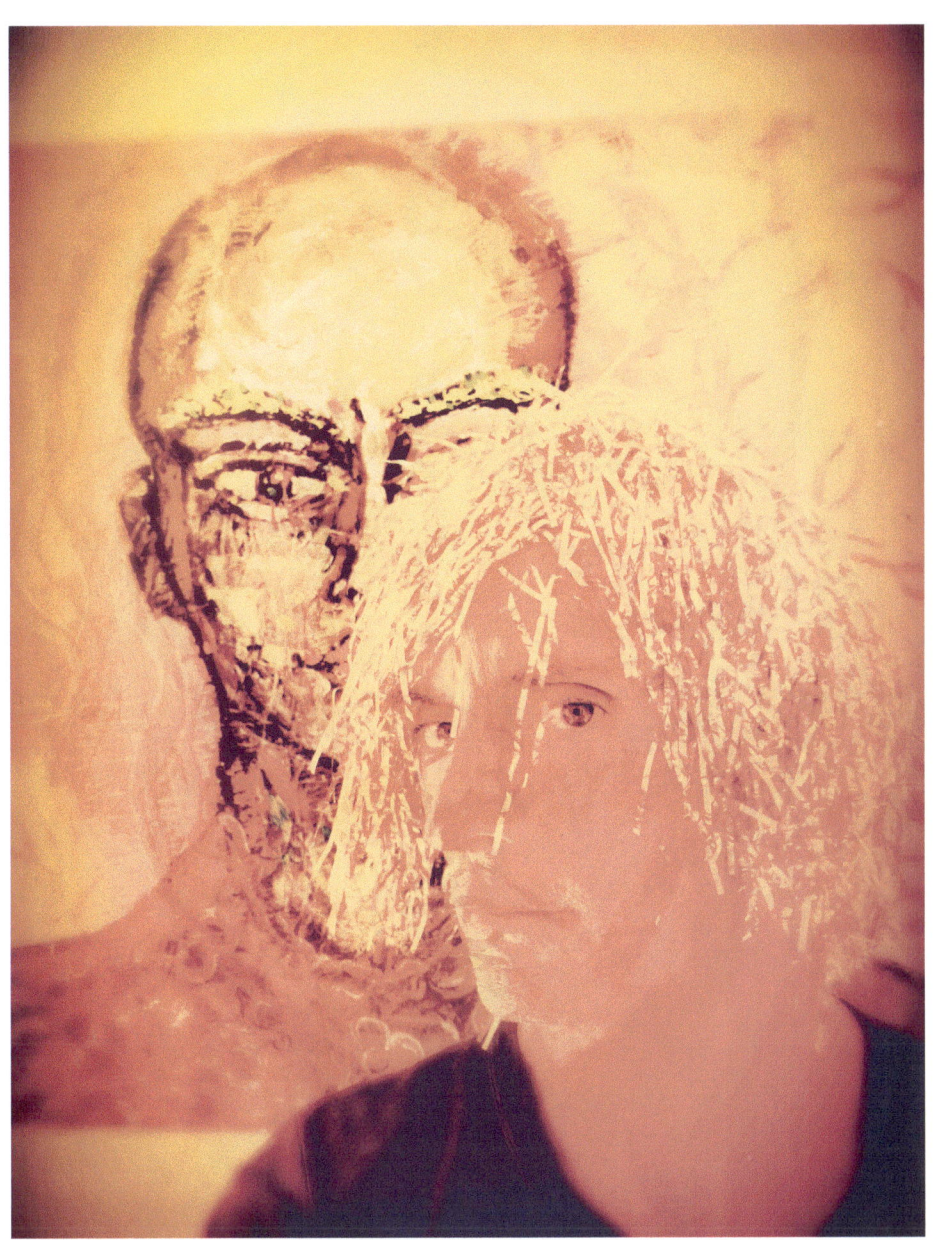

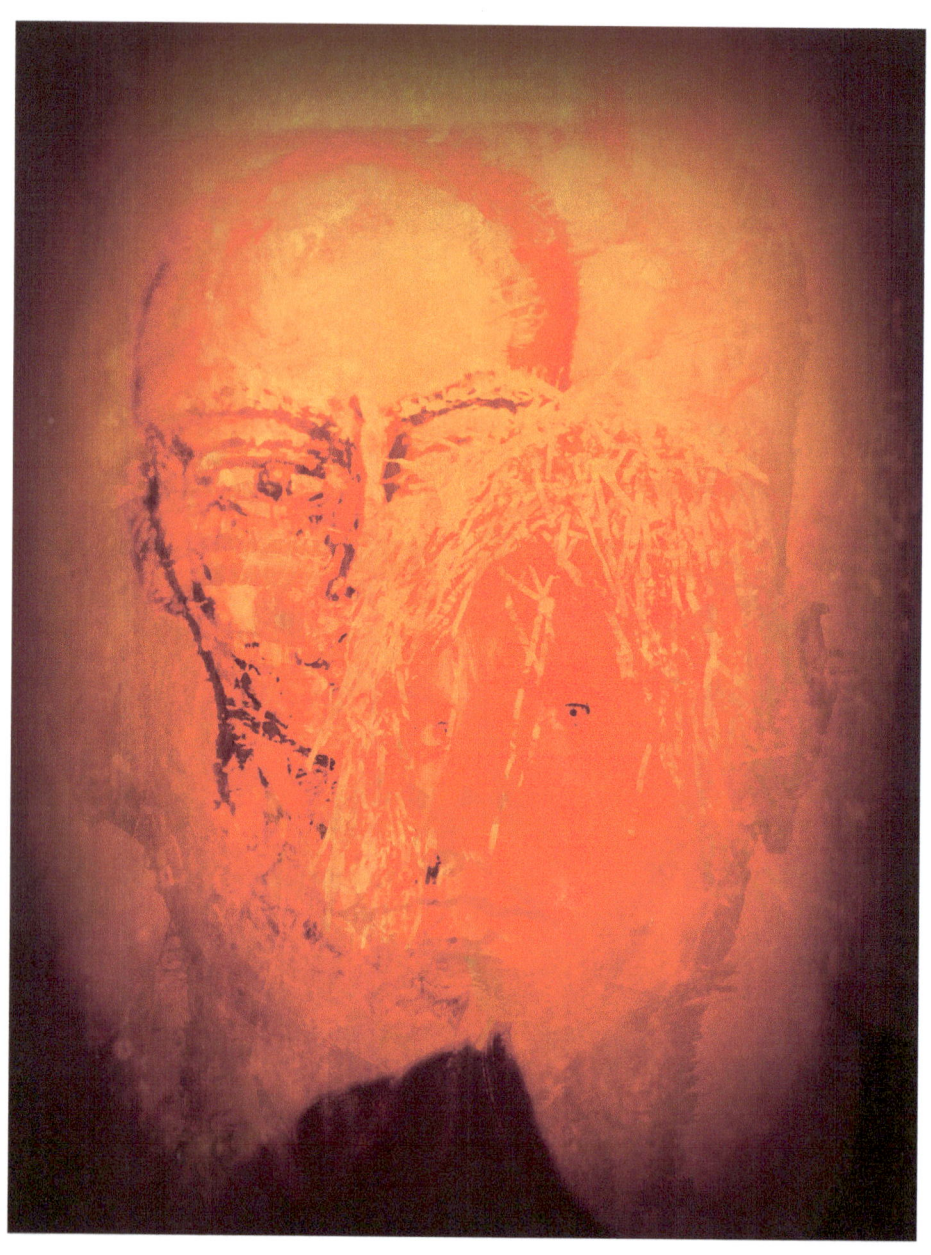

34

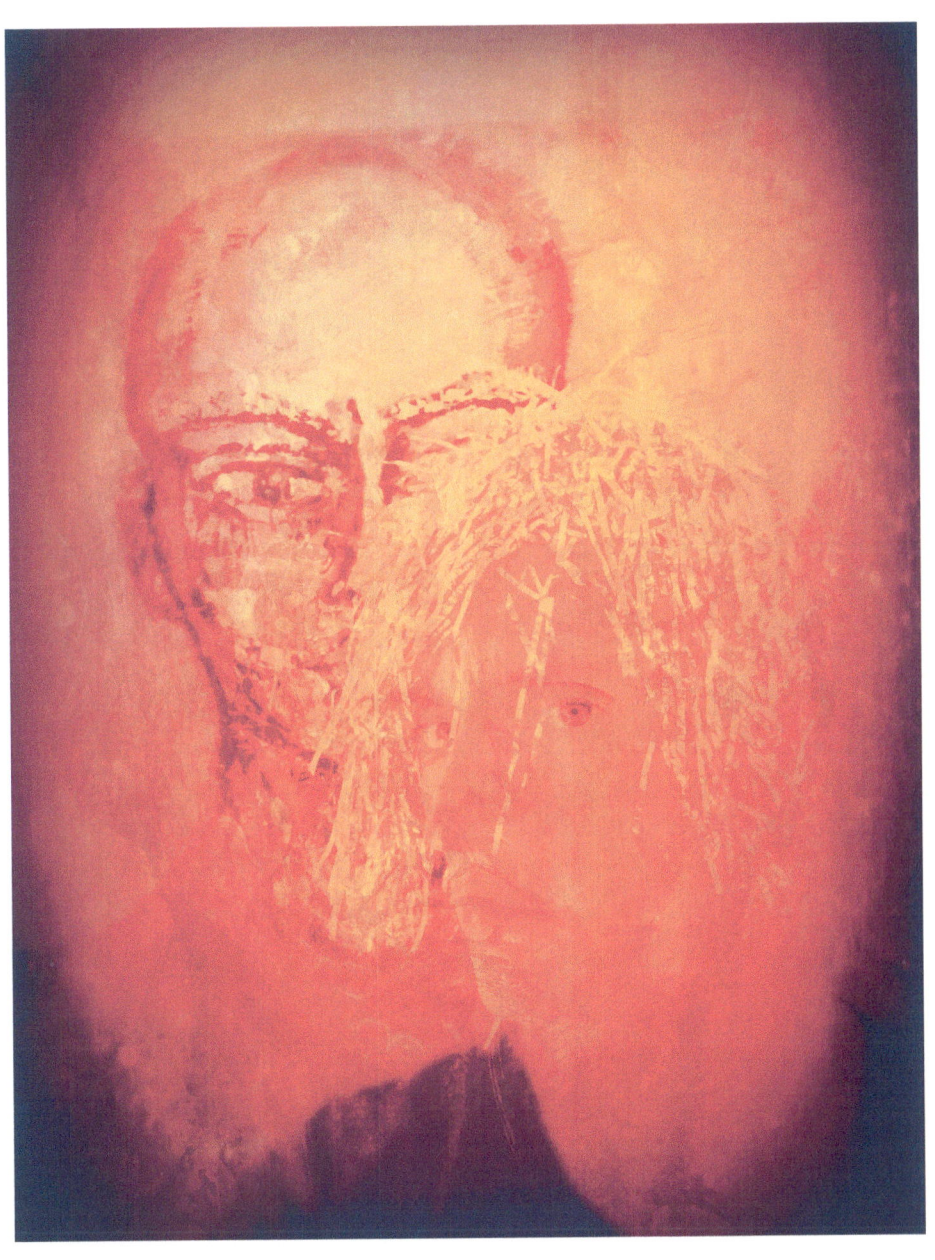

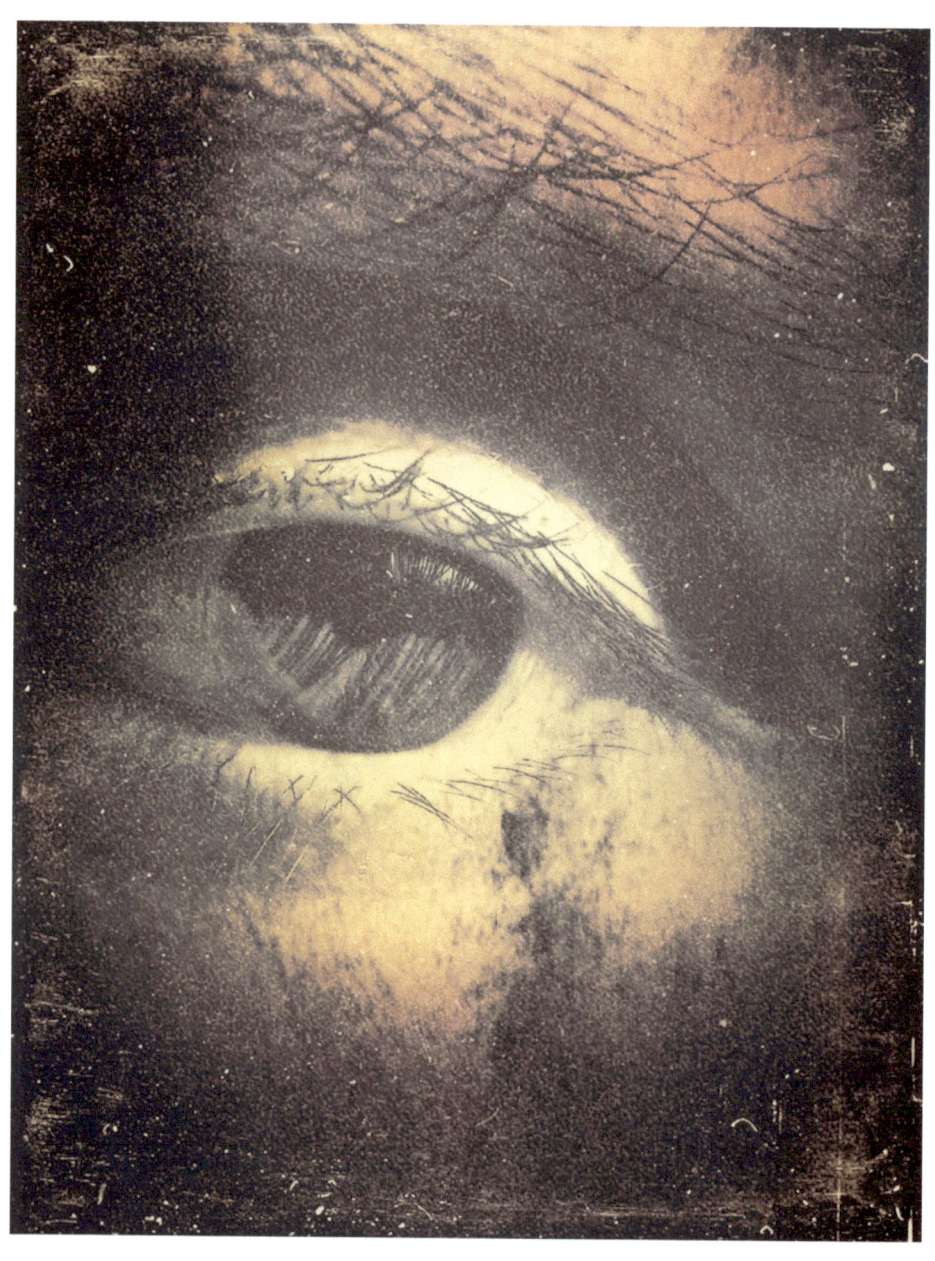

36

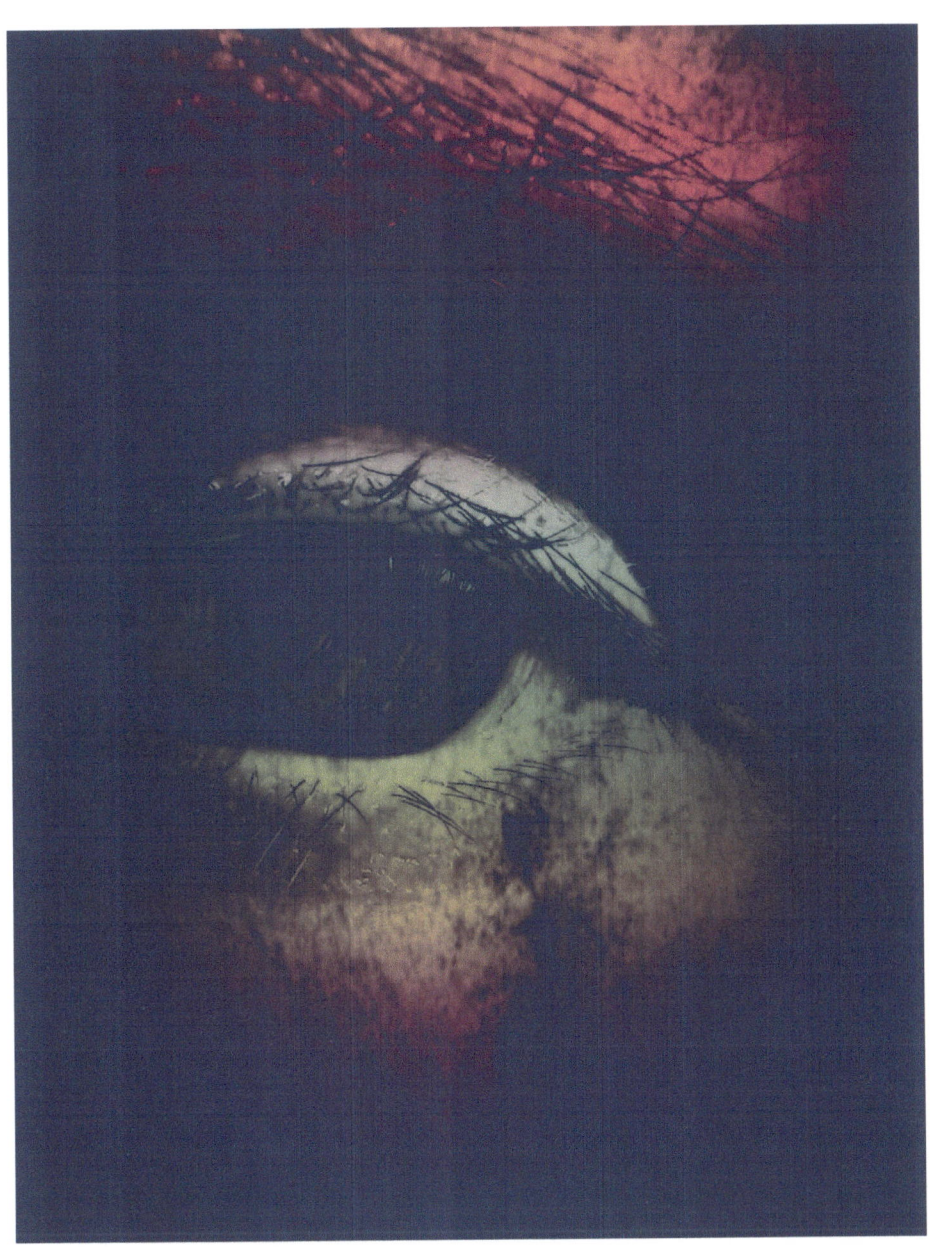

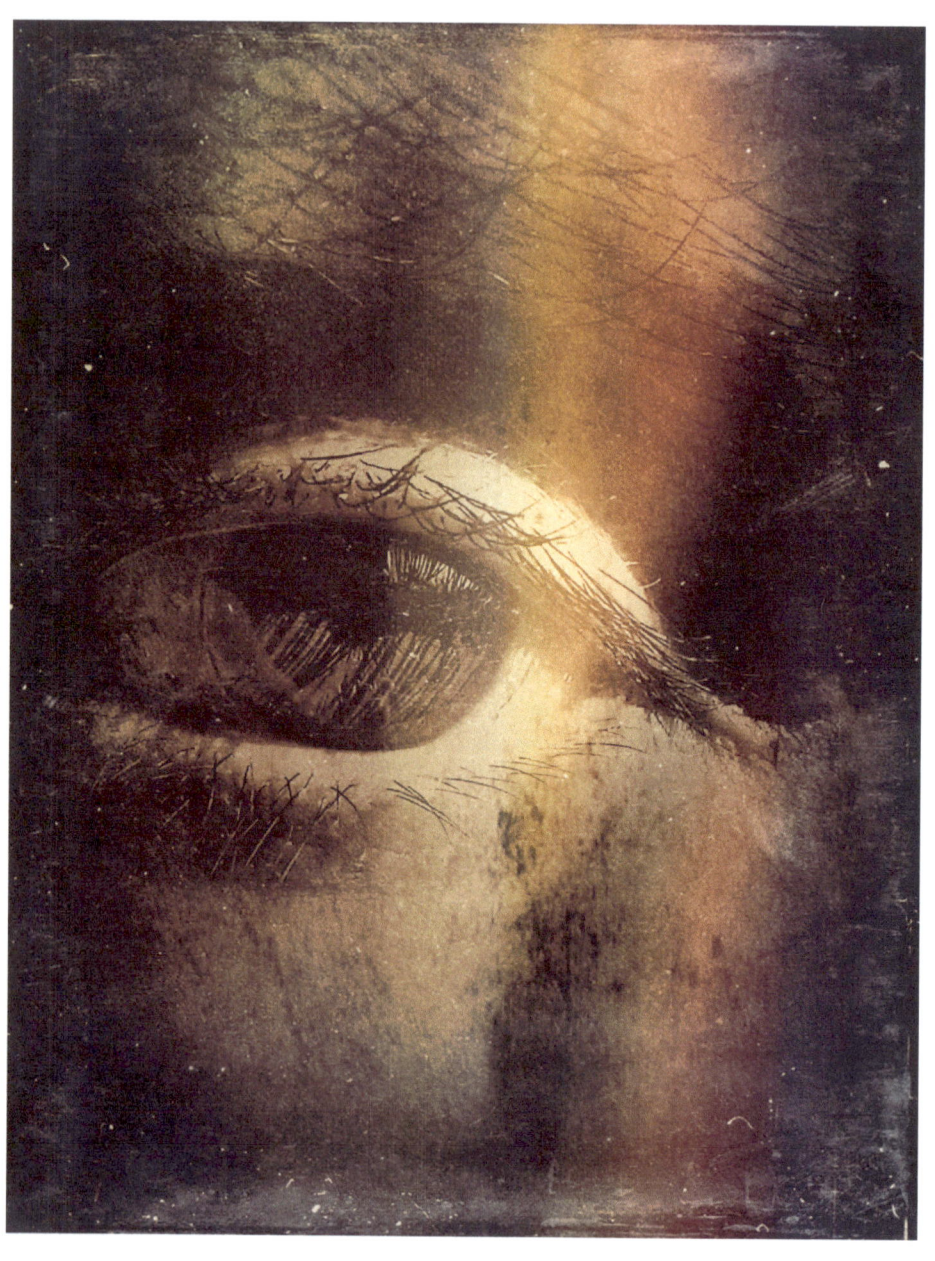

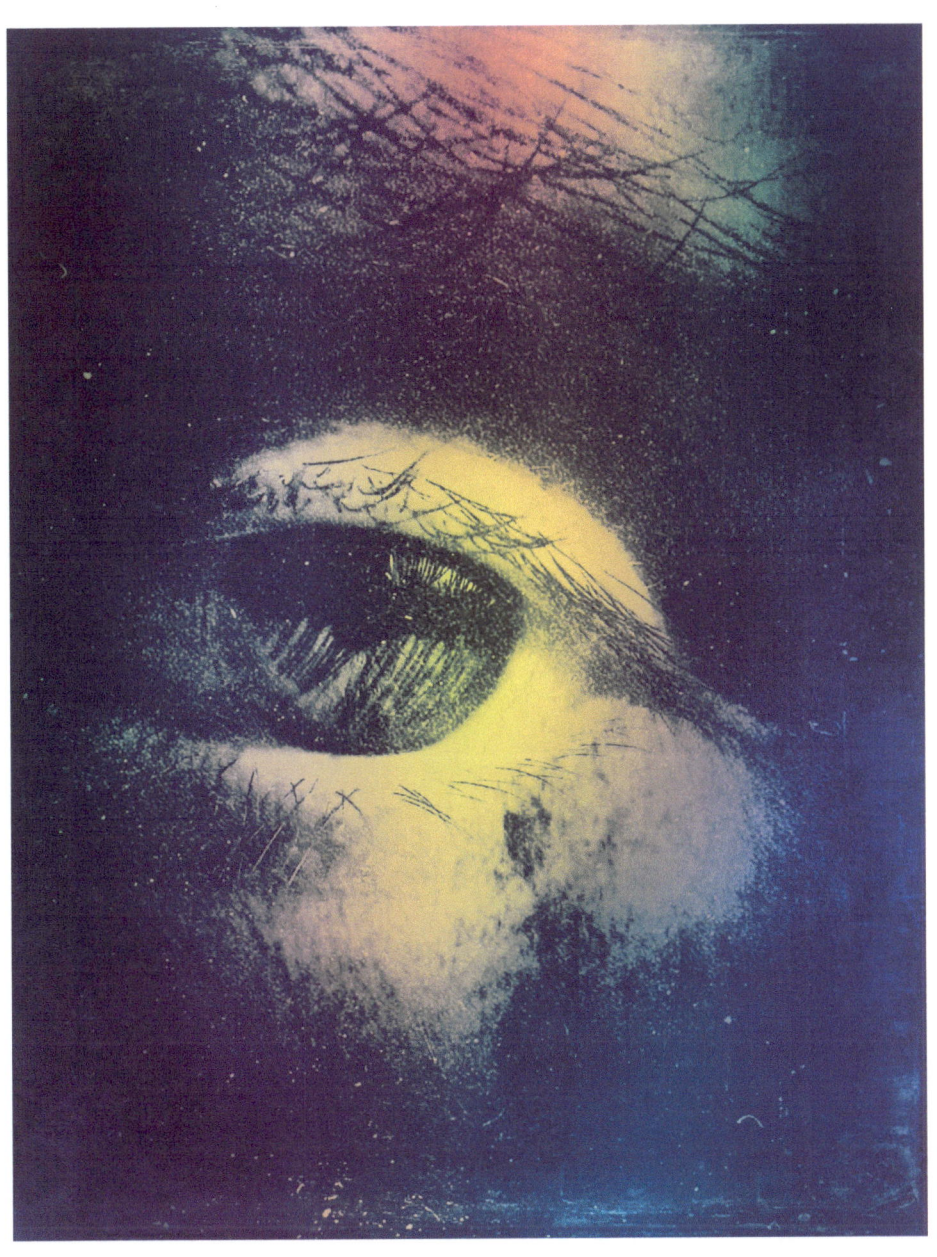

39

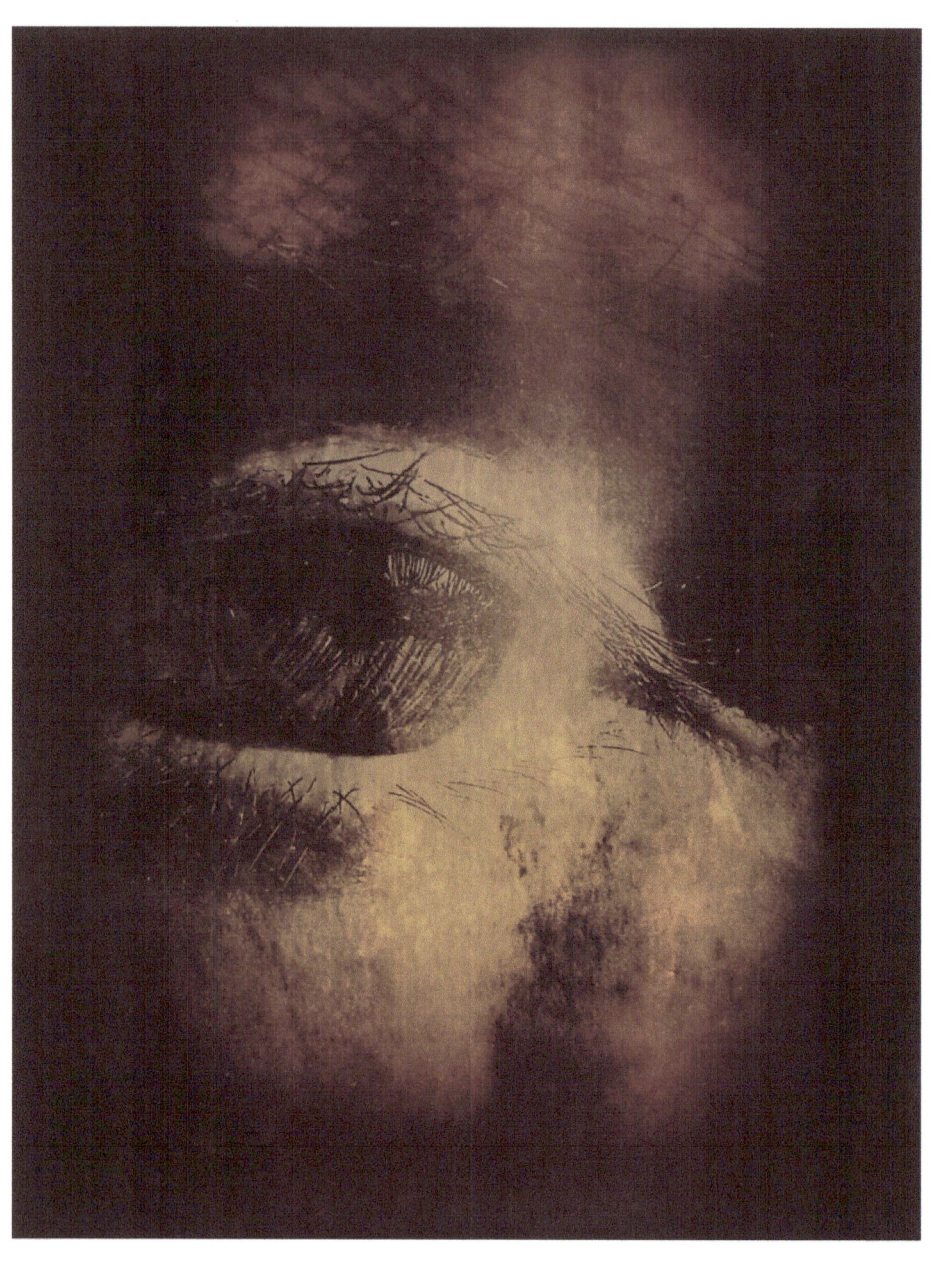

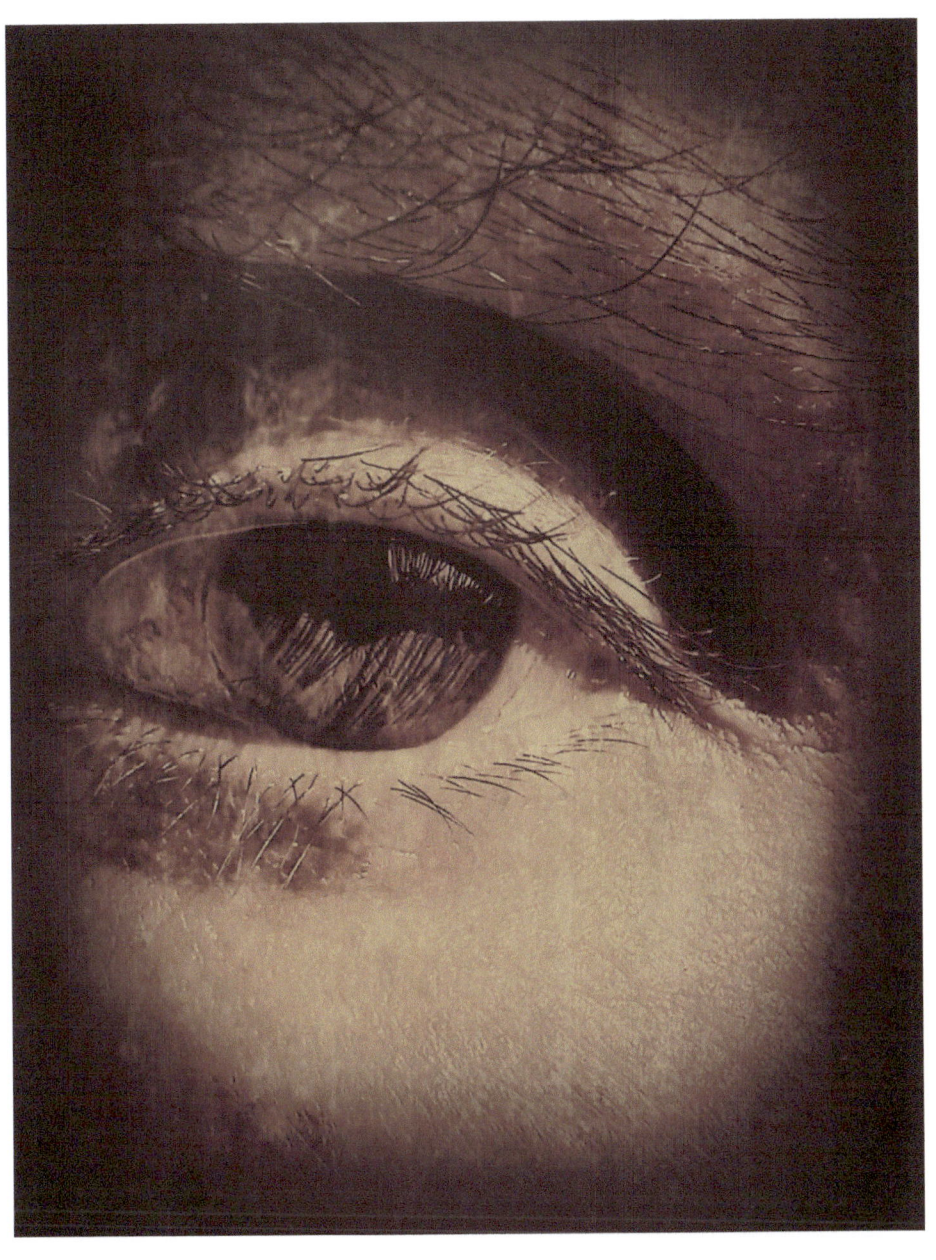

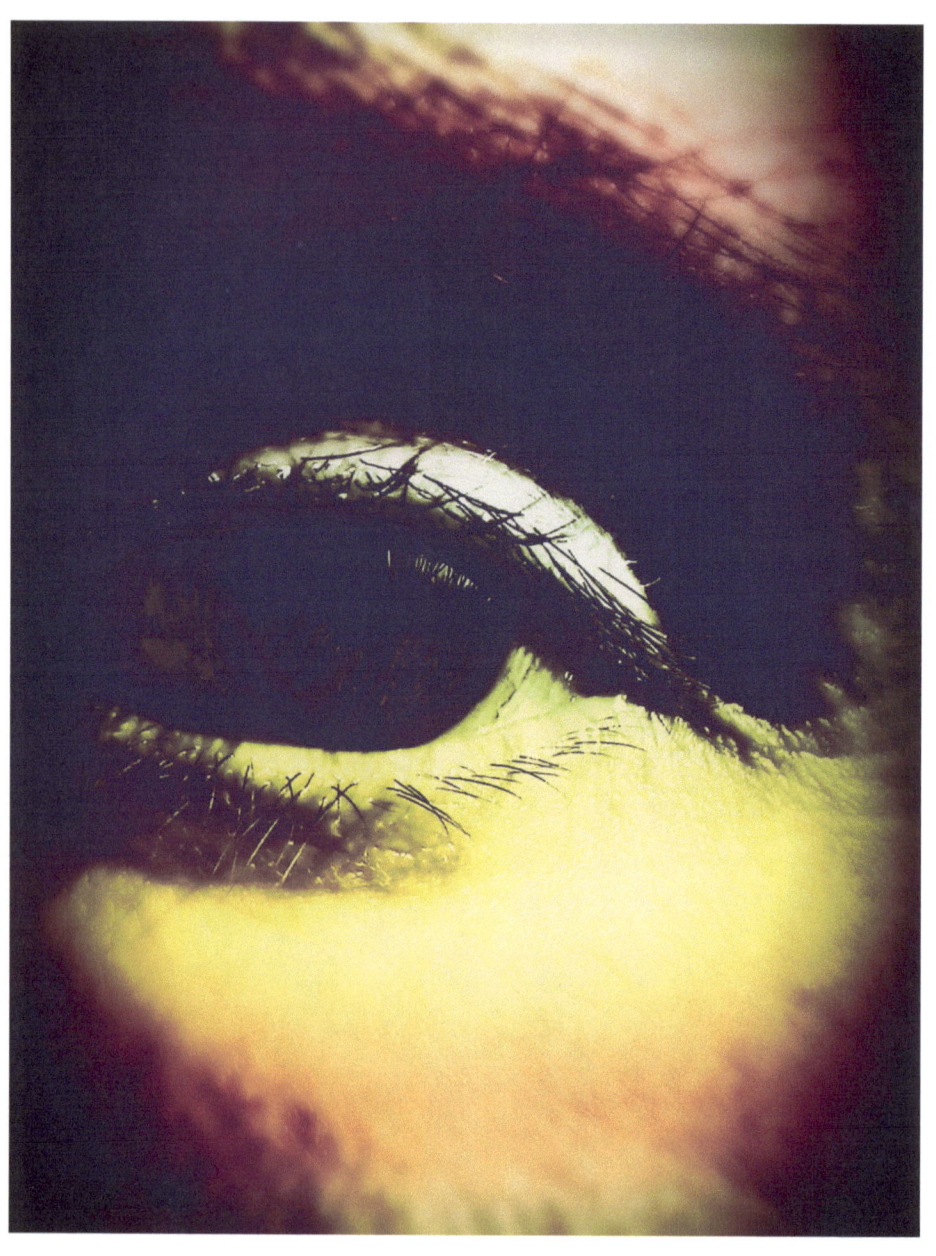

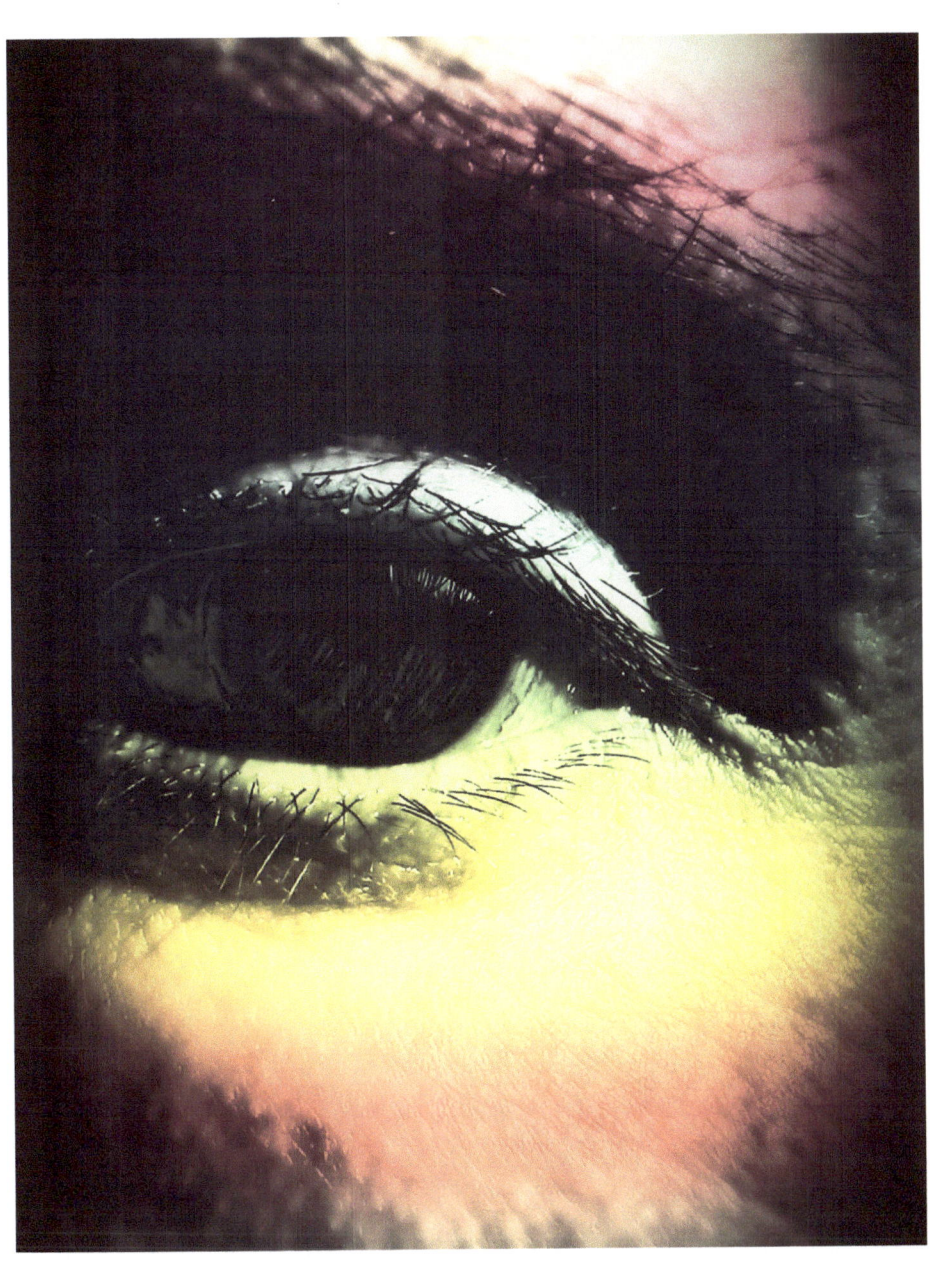

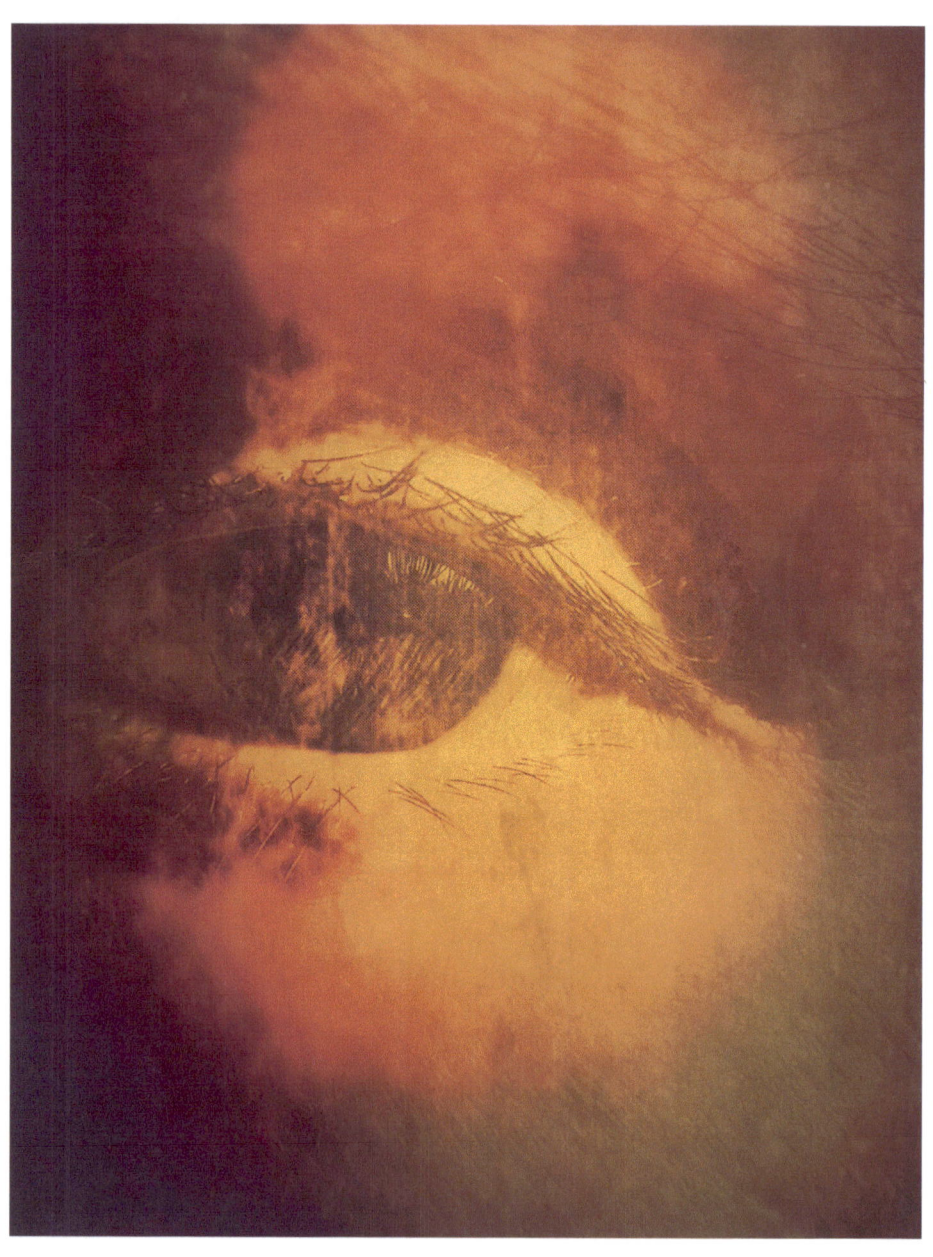

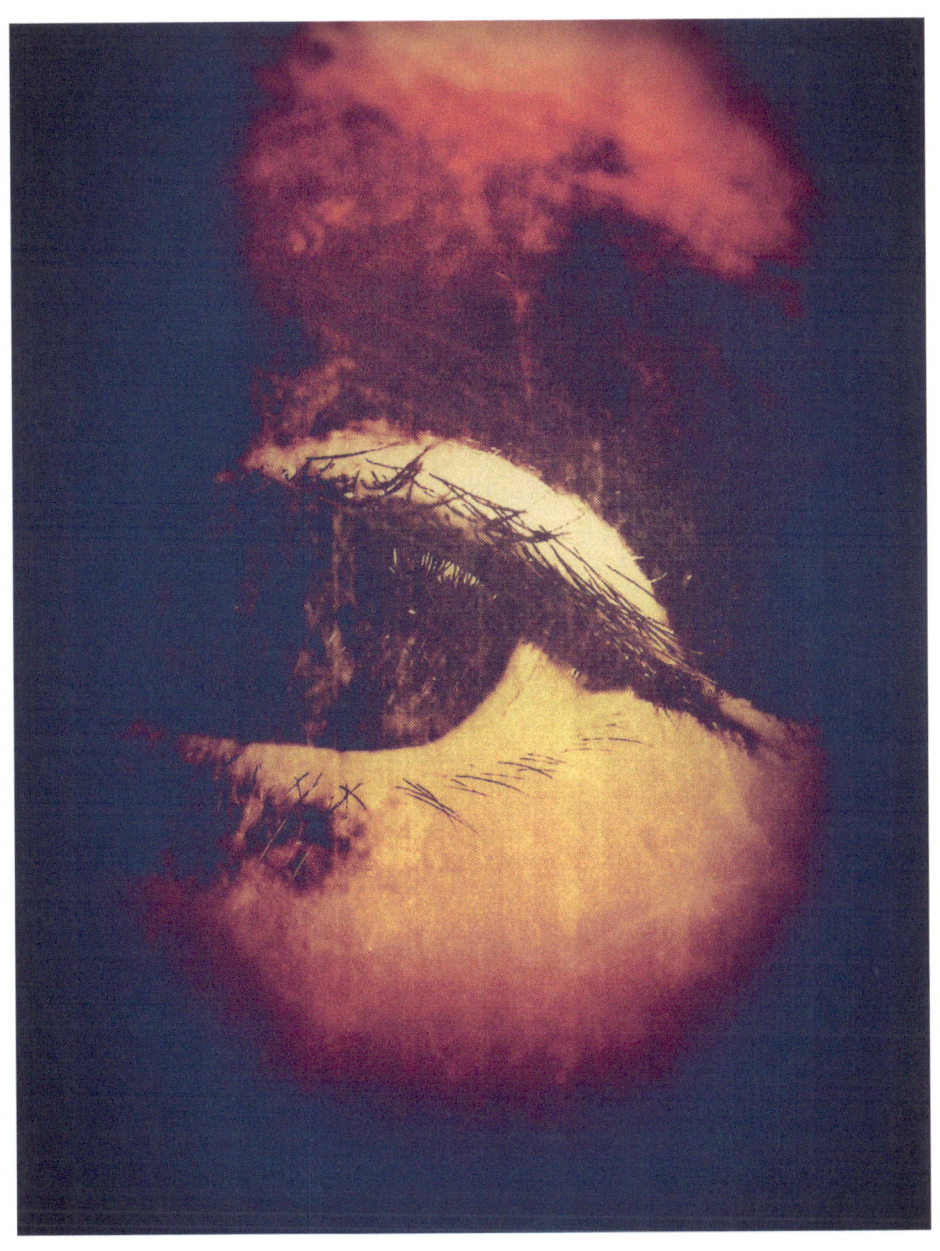

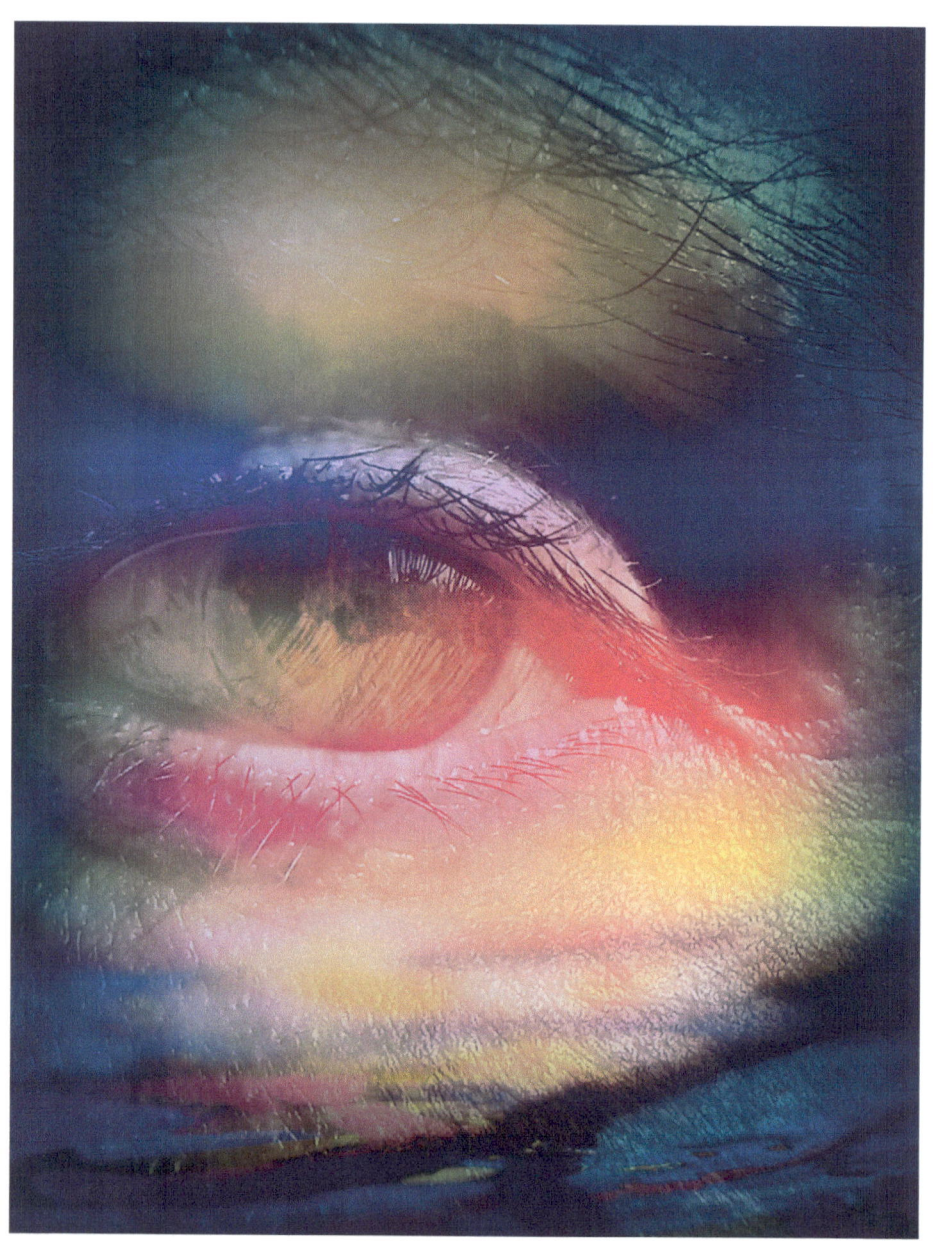

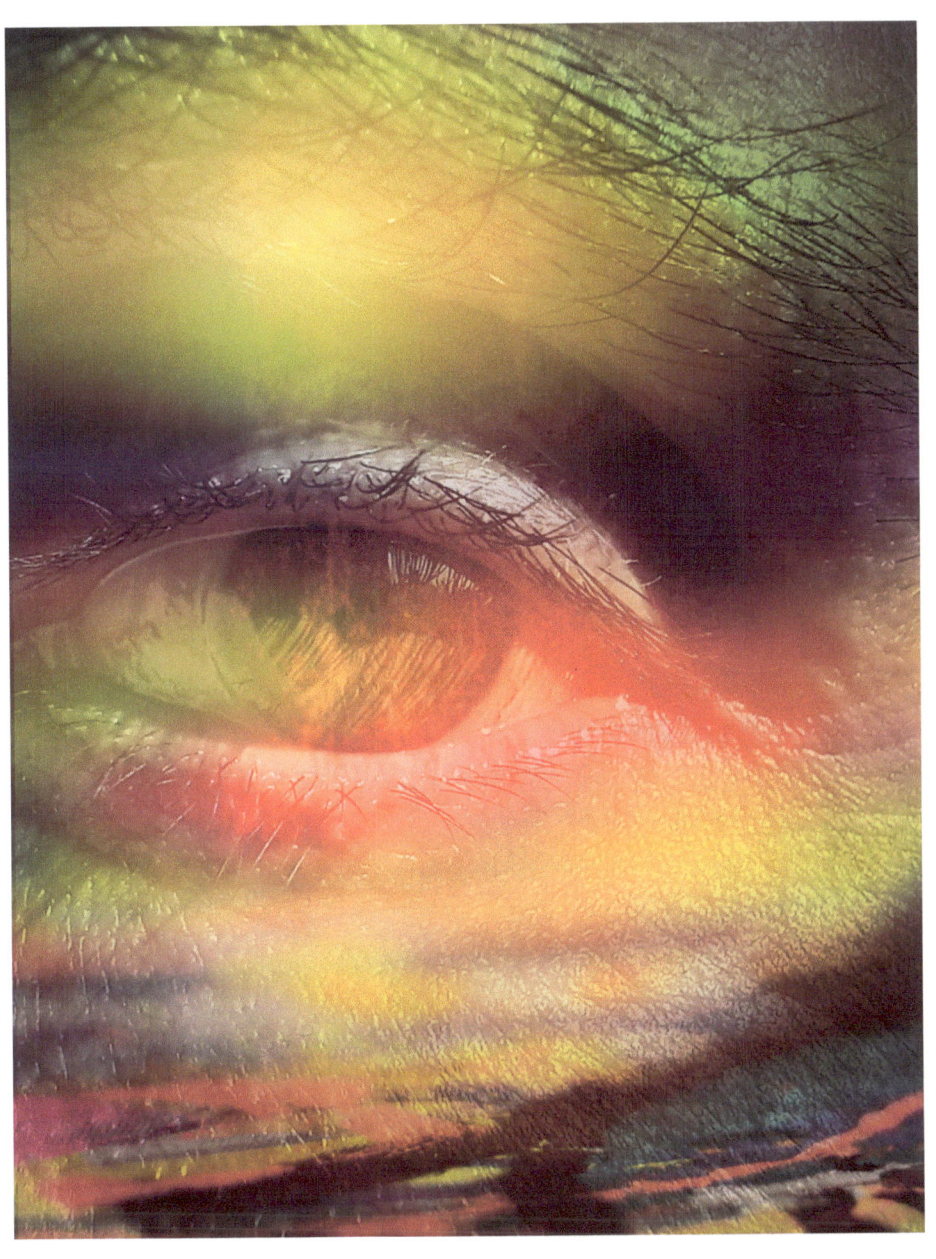

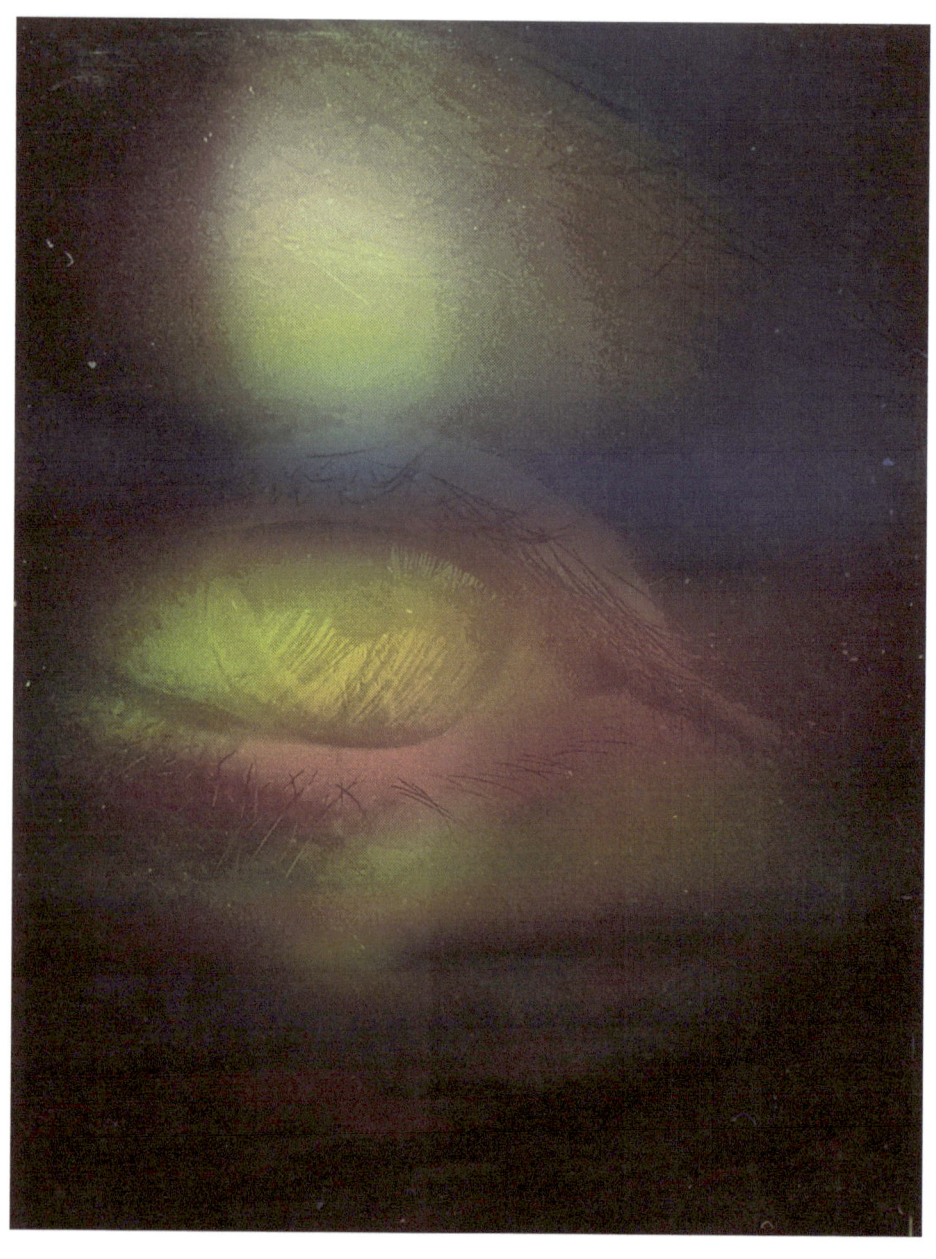

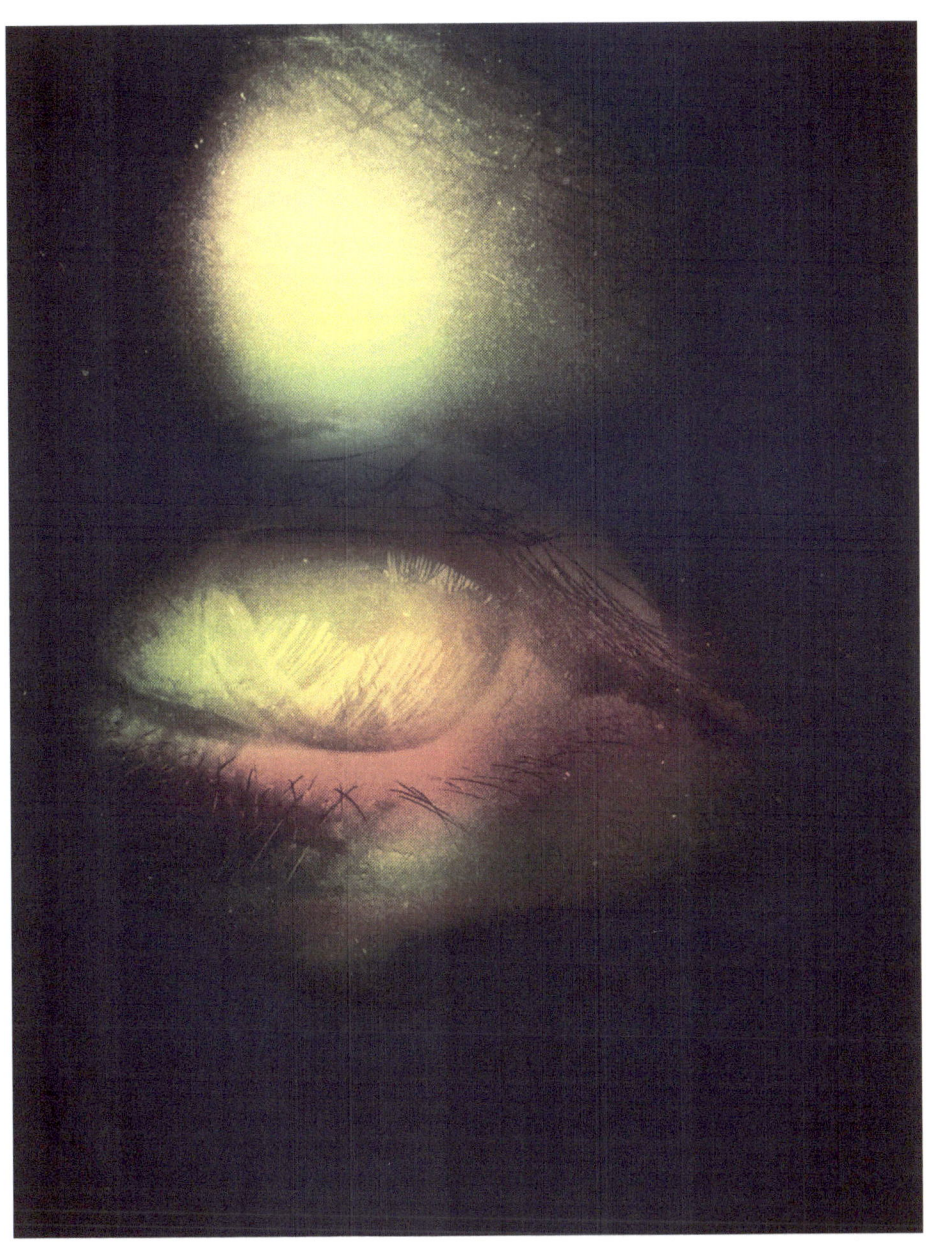

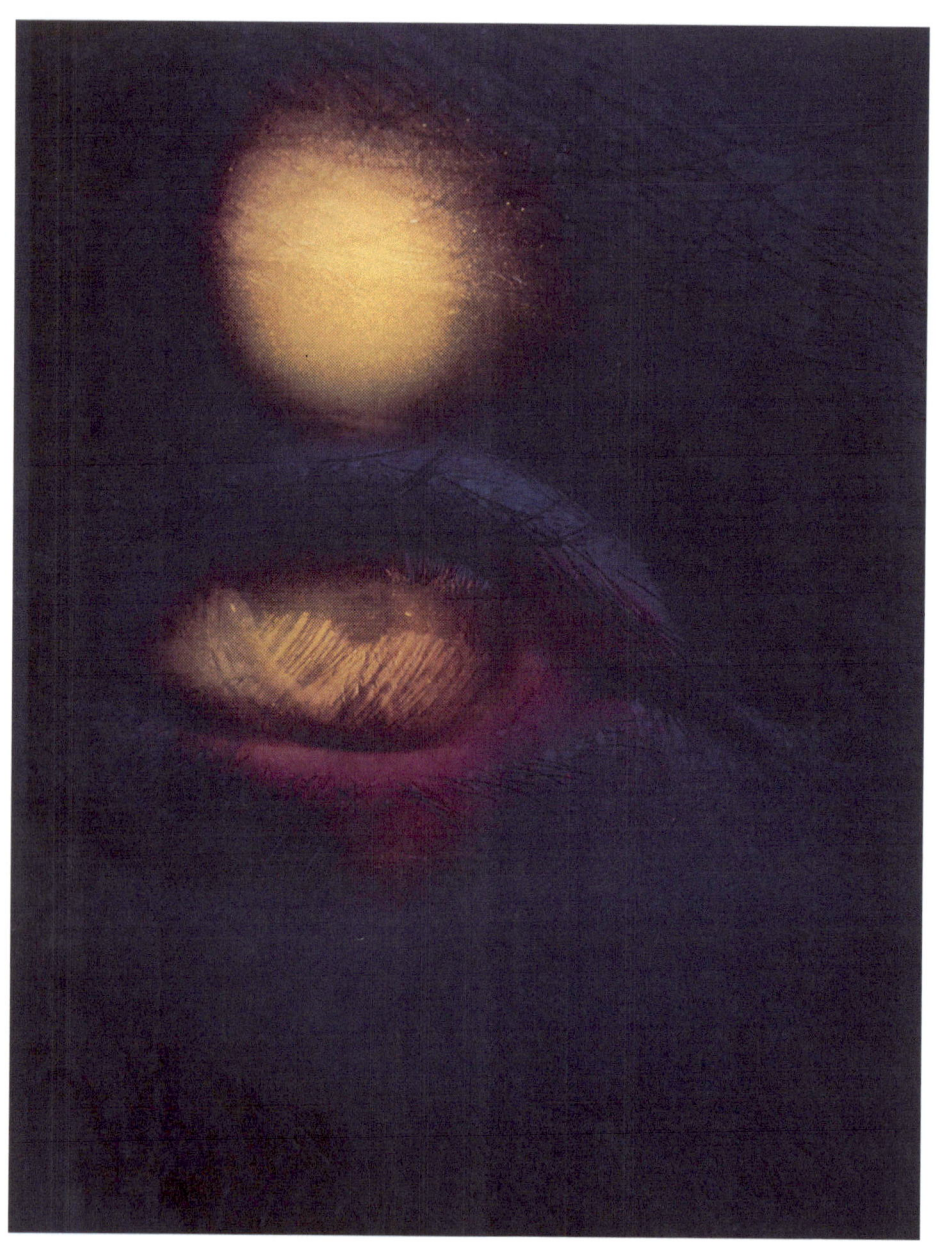

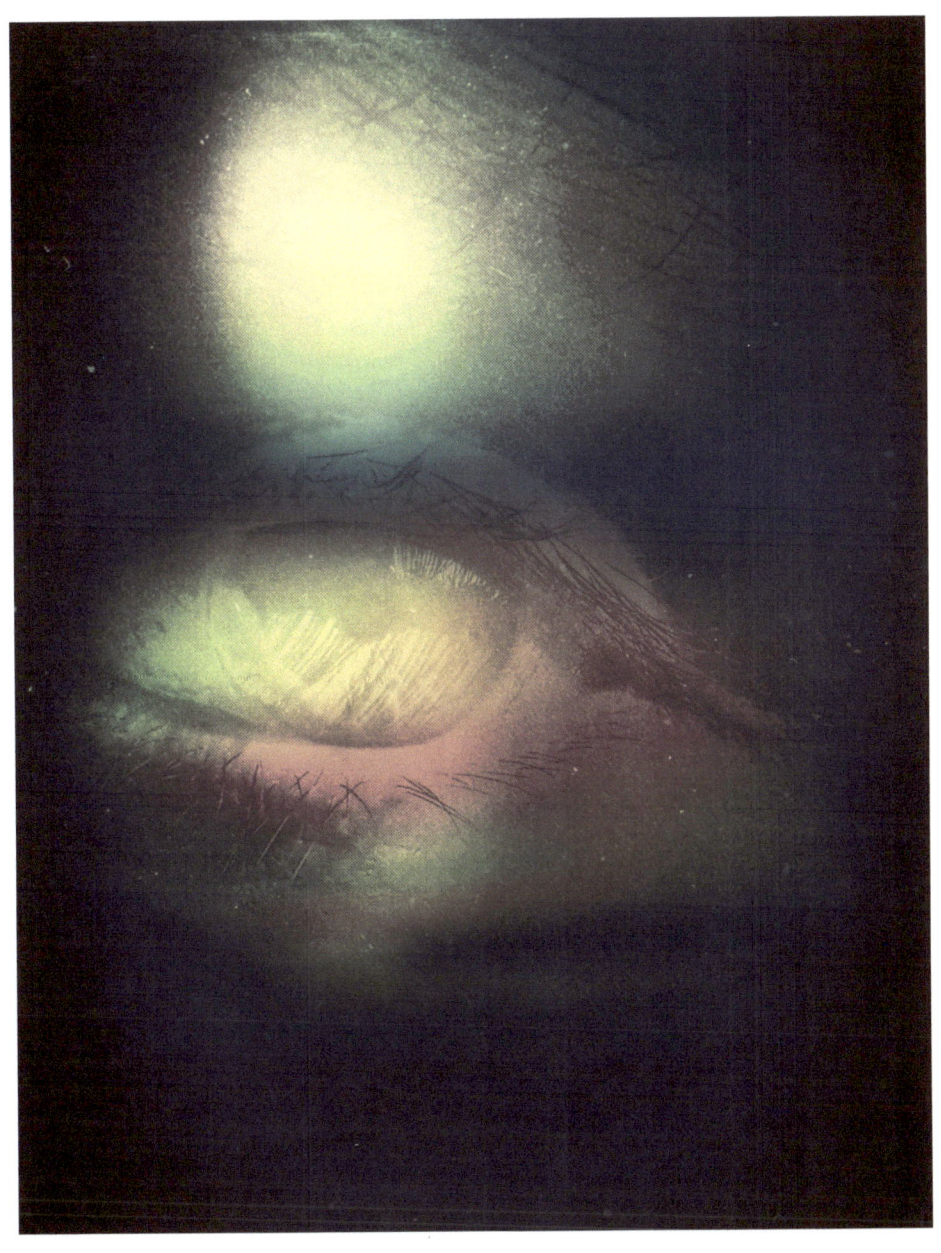

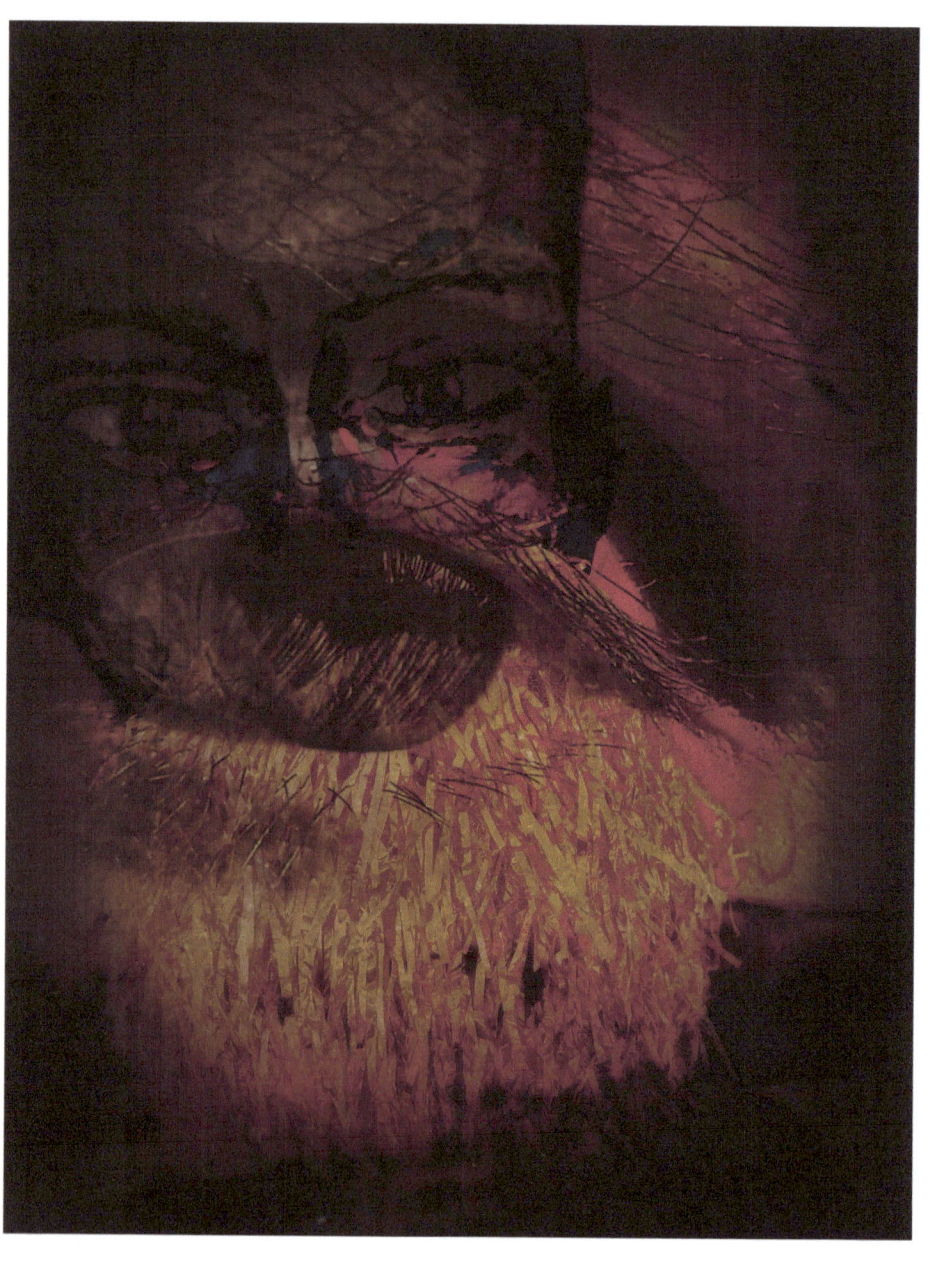

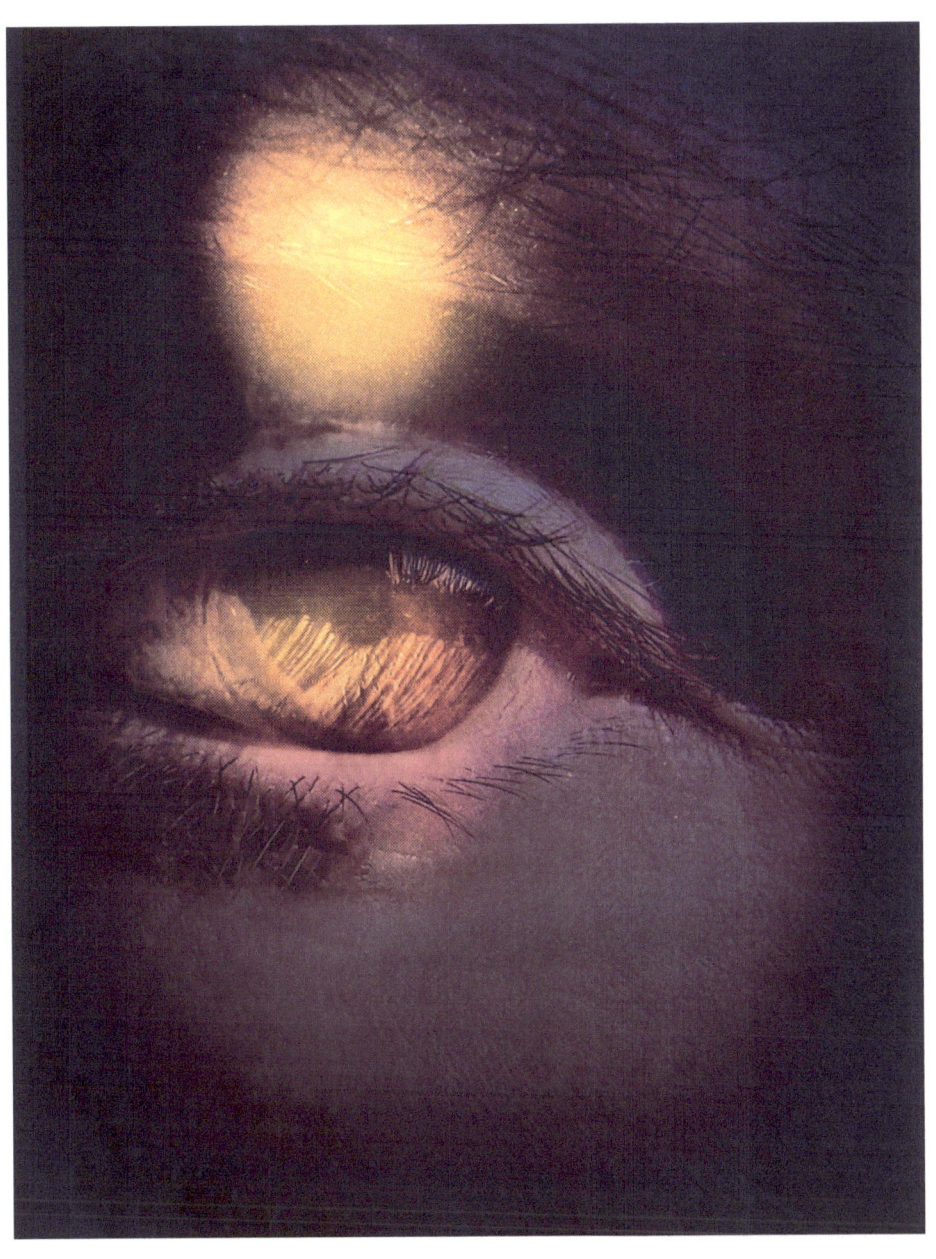

PONDERA VERBORUM ART PROJECT

www.ingramcontent.com/pod-product-compliance
Lightning Source LLC
Chambersburg PA
CBHW050823290526
45792CB00001B/235